Boris's Bus

John Aldridge

Gavin Booth

Stewart J Brown

Hilton Holloway

Keith McGillivray

Matt Prior

James Whiting

Christian Wolmar

Capital Transport

Boris's Bus

This is the story of a period that every reader of it has lived through; a history of a bus that has only just begun. It records the progress of an idea from 2007 for a new bus to the entry into service of the first production vehicles of the design in 2013. It is a story of a project but also of politics; of technical development but also of the teething troubles that often accompany such development. It is told by reference to official documents and also by the words of the people involved with it.

The book team would like to thank (in alphabetical order) Johor Ali, Katy Harris, Sir Peter Hendy, Hilton Holloway, Pieter Lesage, Jamie Martin, Alan Millar, Simon Paterson, Alan Ponsford, Marek Reichman, Ann Reinking, Antony Roskoss, David Stewart, Toby Tinsley, Peter Waller and all those who assisted anonymously. No information for this book has been supplied by any TfL staff illustrated. Thanks also of course go to Boris Johnson, without whom the bus and therefore this book would not exist.

Designed by James Whiting and Lucy Frontani

First published 2013

ISBN 978-1-85414-369-3

Published by Capital Transport Publishing Ltd
www.capitaltransport.com

Printed by Parksons Graphics

BORIS JOHNSON'S PLEDGE

JAMES WHITING

While speaking in September 2007 about the following May's London mayoral elections, Boris Johnson announced that if selected as Conservative party candidate and subsequently elected, he would hold a competition to design a 'new Routemaster' and also replace the bendy buses that had been introduced during the time Ken Livingstone was mayor. The bendy buses were unpopular with motorists and cyclists, while Routemasters had been reduced to operating on two special 'heritage' routes since last running in normal passenger service in December 2005.

In his 2008 manifesto, Johnson included a pledge to introduce what he called a '21st Century Routemaster' to London's streets, saying that he wanted to 'once again give London an iconic bus' that Londoners could be proud of. He confirmed he would commission a competition 'for the world's best designers and engineers to design a brand-new Routemaster that is fully compliant with EU legislation, has disabled access and is run on green fuel'. He coupled this with a promise that when routes operated by bendy buses came up for contract renewal, he would specify that different types of bus would have to be used.

Boris's bus promises became a focus of hot debate in the lead up to the mayoral election. Most of the argument was around the cost of his plans. Various figures were quoted, including one of £112m per annum by Transport for London in March 2008 that Boris interpreted, rightly or wrongly, as an attack on his campaign. He was however largely dependent on TfL for cost estimates and conceded the following month that £100m was about right.

The official figures being quoted for the project comprised the cost of conductors and additional buses and drivers to make up the passenger capacity lost by replacing high-capacity bendy buses with double-deck buses. At the time that Boris was publicising his intention of replacing the bendy buses, there were 399 of these in London. To maintain the passenger capacity it was estimated that 620 of any new double-decker would be needed. The estimate of additional costs of £112m per year was made up of 1,736 conductors at £28,000 each per year, 651 extra drivers at £35,000 (both figures including employer's National Insurance and pensions) and £40m a year for the new buses.

In the election, Boris was standing against Labour's Ken Livingstone, who had been mayor since 2000 (when he stood as an independent) and who had been the first person to hold the position. When the election results were announced, Boris Johnson had overtaken Ken's lead in early opinion polls and was declared the winner, having received 53.18% of the final votes compared with 46.82% for Ken. Many saw transport as one of the main contributors to Boris's victory – including his bus pledges, a crackdown on illegal minicabs and his promise to reverse an unpopular extension of the congestion charge into inner west London that Ken Livingstone had introduced.

With a majority of around 140,000, Boris became mayor and in consequence what might have been just a dream for a new bus for London became a reality. Whether that reality would extend to more than the eight prototype buses that were built depended on the result of the following election, in 2012, when Boris once again stood against Ken. Boris of course pledged to build a fleet of the new buses if re-elected; Ken had other ideas. Boris had become a popular mayor, generating much affection by being a politician who was quite often politically incorrect and projecting an image of not taking himself too seriously. To some extent Ken had achieved popularity for the same qualities. However, it seems possible that the popular pledge on the 'new Routemaster' swung it for Boris, who won the 2012 contest, albeit with a reduced majority of 62,500. Outside London, new jobs in the bus industry depended on that result, leading to the unusual occurrence of celebrations across the Irish Sea around the result of a London mayoral election.

So, because of its origins, the New Bus for London (in official terminology), Boris Bus, New Routemaster, Borismaster or whatever you want to call it, became a very political issue and whether or not someone was in favour of the bus was very often determined by whether or not they were in favour of Boris. On the question of whether the bus represents good value for money, opinions are still sharply divided. Alongside considered and informed opinions, there has been much strongly biased comment.

At this early stage, however, it is not really possible to argue one way or the other on the wisdom or otherwise, in financial terms, of producing the bus. The verdict will largely depend on how many buses are eventually built, both for London and elsewhere, and how long they see service in the capital. It can also be argued that the cost of the bus is not the main issue. Boris made a pledge and he kept it. The people of London voted for a new hop on, hop off, replacement for the Routemaster and they have one.

THE DESIGN COMPETITION

CHRISTIAN WOLMAR

The promise of a New Bus for London was prompted by nostalgia and a desire to keep alive the idea of the iconic Routemaster. This reverence for the Routemaster rather ignored its real history. When it was first introduced, the Routemaster was notoriously unreliable, with many breakdowns and with automatic gearboxes that gave a jerky ride. These problems took some time to overcome before the Routemaster came to be regarded as a reliable bus with a classic design. Apart from a couple of heritage routes, the 9 and the 15, the last Routemasters in London had run in December 2005. Ken Livingstone, who first became mayor in 2000, had originally supported retaining the buses, which were much loved by Londoners and tourists alike, but realised that with the extensive use of Oyster cards, the expense of keeping the old buses going and, crucially, the lack of access for disabled passengers and buggies, they should be phased out.

Then politics entered into the story. In September 2007, the Conservative mayoral candidate, Boris Johnson, trailing in the polls at the time, announced that he would support a competition for a new bus for London based on Routemaster principles, most notably an open platform at the back. This attracted considerable attention, not all of which was positive. *Autocar* magazine's Hilton Holloway recalls:

'The strength of the condemnations of Johnson's policy of commissioning a new bus spurred me into action to help. One evening in October 2007 I was lamenting at the *Autocar* office what I saw as the remarkable narrowness of vision in the opposition to a bespoke London bus. I told my two bosses that I was sure I could procure a design to prove the nay-sayers wrong. I was given four pages in the Christmas issue and told to get on with it. I knew where to go for a new bus proposal: Alan Ponsford, boss of the bus and truck designer Capoco. Ponsford very quickly accepted my emailed challenge and – with just a single face-to-face meeting at the Institute of Mechanical Engineers – his team produced the beautiful cutaway design that was shown to Johnson and featured in *Autocar*, as well as *The Times*, on the BBC and elsewhere. Showing Johnson the cutaway engineering illustrations, my only political advice was to not let anyone tell him it couldn't be done, because it could.'

Called the RMXL, Ponsford's design concept was a low-floor bus with a lightweight aluminium space frame that incorporated disabled access through a closing front door behind the front wheels. There was, too, an open-platform rear access, leading directly on to the staircase at the back. *Autocar* had paid Capoco a modest £750 for the design.

Johnson liked the idea in principle and he suggested that he would hold a formal design competition to develop a new Routemaster if he won the May 2008 election. It formed a significant part of his manifesto which also focused on scrapping the bendy buses introduced while Ken Livingstone was mayor; these

The cutaway engineering drawing of Alan Ponsford's 9.8 metre RMXL as it appeared in the Christmas 2007 issue of *Autocar* magazine.

had also suffered severe teething problems, notably a series of fires. These had been remedied and the buses were running efficiently along the main arterial corridors, but some Londoners felt the bendy buses were inappropriate for the narrow streets in central London. They were also regarded as a free service for fare dodgers who did not have to walk past the driver to get on the bus and therefore could avoid using the Oyster reader. Consequently, the political message conveyed by Johnson was that these 'alien' bendy buses would be got rid of to be replaced by an 'iconic' – a word that later became overused in the debate – new Routemaster.

In July 2008, Johnson announced the competition for the new bus with the aim of involving both the industry and the public at large. He called for the new bus design to be 'stylish, spacious and energy efficient' and with an open platform at the back staffed by a second crew member. As part of paying prize money to the winners and runners up, Transport for London purchased the copyright in the designs, permitting the royalty-free use of elements from them in the final design. There were three categories: Whole Design, Design Element and 'Imagine', the last named allowing creative minds to run free without constraints of practicality. The Imagine section was divided into four age groups: Below 11, 11-15, 16-18 and adult. A number of children sent in entries.

The judging panel, overseen by the Mayor, was made up of the Mayor's transport adviser Kulveer Ranger, Transport Commissioner Peter Hendy, TfL's MD of Surface Transport David Brown, London Buses' managers Mike Weston and Clare Kavanagh and bus design consultant David Quainton, formerly marketing director of Alexander Dennis. Quainton's job (unpaid; expenses only) was to sort through the 700-odd entries to decide which ones were worth showing to the rest of the judges. He scored each of the Design entries according to such things as style, innovation, good use of interior space and practicality and making sure they met the specifications that had been laid down. For the Imagine category, the specifications did not apply. The Imagine category called for the submission of imaginative ideas without too much regard for practicality. The Design category was more specific and asked for detailed designs of a low floor red double-decker bus with at least one internal staircase, a rear open platform, and one other entrance with doors, to be crewed by a driver and conductor, and suitable for carrying at least 72 passengers seated and standing. A maximum length of 13.5m was specified and the bus could have up to three axles. It had to be practical and economic and capable of being put into mass production. The competition offered cash prizes for entrants, with £25,000 for the winner, and smaller awards for good ideas in the Imagine category – a total of £80,000.

There were still doubts about whether this was a serious attempt to create a new bus for the capital or whether it was just a sophisticated PR exercise. However, the response, with 225 entries for the Design category and a further 475 in the Imagine category, by the closing date of 19th September 2008 was very enthusiastic. Many of the designs that had been submitted to the competition were of a very high standard and incorporated a number of innovative features.

The results were announced just before Christmas 2008 with the £25,000 prize for the key Design category being shared between Capoco and a joint submission made by architects Foster and Partners and the car manufacturer Aston Martin. The Aston Martin-Foster bus design envisaged a highly-manoeuvrable, zero-emissions 71-seater vehicle, with solar panels built into a polycarbonate-glazed roof, full accessibility, warm lighting and wooden floors. According to Foster, the design was finalised 'after an intense period of research which included canvassing opinion from passengers, drivers and conductors' with the aim of designing 'a new bus from the inside-out'. The Capoco design combined a low flat floor to allow easy access but retaining the Routemaster-style front engine and open rear platform. It had room for 80 passengers, 66 of which were seated.

Alan Ponsford in his Capoco Design studio with his entry contrasted with a Routemaster. His design sought to repeat the lightweight approach of the original with a target unladen weight of 8,200kg.

Foster + Partners with Aston Martin win joint first prize in competition to design a new bus for London

19.12.2008

The joint submission by Foster + Partners and Aston Martin has won first prize, alongside Capoco Design, in Transport for Londons competition to design a new bus for the capital. The two iconic British brands worked together to challenge preconceptions of bus design with a vehicle that is environmentally sensitive, accessible, convivial and reinvents a much-loved symbol of London for the modern era.

After an intense period of research which included canvassing opinion from passengers, drivers and conductors, the two parties worked in close collaboration to design a new bus from the inside-out. In doing so, consideration was given to a wide range of issues including layout, use of materials, motive power, passenger experience and the bus impact on the streetscape and the environment of the city. The bus is designed to navigate the dense and varied streets of London, employing innovative technologies to allow for greater manoeuvrability and energy conservation. Optimising safety, the driver's cabin provides panoramic views as well as incorporating screens to supervise CCTV images and radio communications with the on-board conductor.

Much like a car or a building, the design evolved in response to the needs of its users. The layout, lighting and wooden floors are conceived to encourage a spirit of warmth and community. The arrangement of the decks is driven by comfort and particular consideration is given to the selection of reconstituted leather upholstery to create a tactile living room feel, especially in the saloon-like lower deck.

The new bus is zero emissions ready, accessible for all and will set new standards for sustainable public service vehicles. Passengers benefit from views from the top of the deck through a glazed roof which incorporates solar cells to generate energy and filter daylight to control the temperature inside.

The bus design re-introduces the rear open access platform that made London's Routemaster bus so popular up until its withdrawal from general service. This is supplemented by a side door to facilitate access for the mobility impaired and families with young children.

Lord Foster said:
I am delighted that we have won joint first prize with the Aston Martin/Foster + Partners design. This project has really captured my imagination. Londons buses are so much a part of the essence of this city functionally, symbolically and geographically. They help us draw a mental map their destinations are Londons historic places, often green: Shepherds Bush, Islington Green, Hampstead Heath, Green Park. Our design seeks to combine contemporary innovation with timelessness. Like the original Routemaster which was ahead of its time and consequently endured a new bus for London should establish a whole new travel experience that espouses 21st century aspirations, while celebrating the memory and the experience of the original.

Foster + Partners in association with Aston Martin won first prize jointly with Capoco, whose design is seen opposite. The team of Foster and Aston Martin came up with the kind of style Boris Johnson was looking for and, though totally new to bus design, did a lot of homework to produce an attractive proposal with a number of practical features. Their press release from the time is shown here. The bus would have been powered by a hydrogen fuel cell that would charge batteries distributed within the lower floor construction. It would have zero emissions and be almost silent in operation. It was also designed to be easily upgradable to alternative power units as technology developed. By using electric wheel hub motors, the axle-free design envisaged a low floor throughout the length of the lower deck. How practical all this may have been is open to question. The majority of the lower saloon seats were longitudinal, including two tip-up seats in the wheelchair area. Upstairs at the rear a quarter-circle seat for three people was placed next to the stairs and would follow the curve of the bus. The roof would incorporate lightweight polycarbonate glazing panels running the length of the upper deck and these would have photo-voltaic panels to help charge the batteries. Solar film on the glazing would help control heat gain. The bus design, with lightweight composite material for its bodywork and sustainable materials like leather and wood for the interior, was 10.7m long and seated 71 people.

One of the competition's entrants, Toby Tinsley, speaks of the task the designers were faced with: 'The function of the bus has to come first. It's not so much about what you can do, it's establishing what you can't do and then trying to make it work. Designing a bus is very different from other vehicles – you can't simply sculpt a beautiful shape around a chassis – there are lots of rules; how many people, front and rear access, disabled access, safety, ease of use and so forth.'

Just as Alan Ponsford won joint first prize with a design he worked on single-handedly, Jamie Martin, seen here at the awards ceremony, won joint second prize for his solo effort on a modern version of the Routemaster (the second row of pictures in this photograph), which he called the London Navigator. It was an early favourite of the judges, who referred to it as a 'bold and modern take on original Routemaster lines'. The bus was designed as a hybrid with rear-axle hub motors. The front entrance for wheelchair users employed plug doors as on London tube trains.

The Hector Serrano Studio, in association with Minarro Garcia and Javier Esteban, was the other joint second prizewinner and its entry was a firm favourite of Boris Johnson's, according to one correspondent who was at the awards ceremony. It too had plug doors at the front for wheelchair users and made reference to the Routemaster in its bonnet and front grille design. The designers aimed to retain the friendly and warm feeling of the RM and it was one of the shortest of the designs submitted, which when coupled with hybrid diesel-electric drive would be low on emissions. The Union Flag patterned wheel covers were a nice touch.

The Routemaster heritage was a feature in many of the designs submitted for the competition. Toby Tinsley and Adrian Dewey had some fundamental things they wanted to push forward in their design – the 'nose' of the bus being one of them. 'A car', said Toby, 'is very recognisable from the shape of the front grille and I wanted to keep the look of the iconic old bus in the new bus, so we took the nose as the starting point and worked back from there. By doing this you strengthen the heritage and familiarity through a modern design'. The sharp diagonal 'strike' on the platform and stairs makes a feature from the internal staircase.

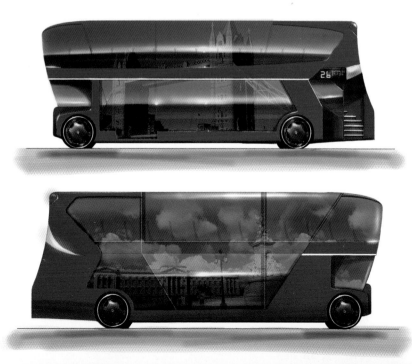

Even in the Design category, some of the designs submitted would have presented serious practical issues. London based designers Pope Wainwright approached the design of their bus 'from the inside out' and it would certainly seem from these illustrations that it would have given good views for its passengers. Glass was envisaged that would reduce solar gain in the summer months and provide some insulation during the winter months, though how effective this would have been is open to question.

Raj Nahal also included a glazed staircase in his design, another one to incorporate a Routemaster style front grille. Behind the nearside front wheel is a second entrance.

15

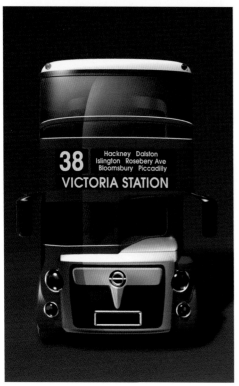

Reiko Ito is a design studio located in Tokyo and Milan. In the area of vehicle design they have worked on cars, some very futuristic looking mobility vehicles and an electrically assisted bicycle. Like many other entrants to the competition, they had not previously designed a bus. Their bus, with a Union Flag pattern in its window layout, had a glazed centre door that projected (along with the window above it) from the main bodywork in a way that made it look articulated and would have given the rest of the bus a restricted width to fit within the legal maximum. The offside handrail may have been a design feature that balanced the platform handrail aesthetically but it does not appear to be of much practical use.

Royal College of Art student Jukka Rautiainen's design was modern, attractive and distinctive. Tube style gates are shown on the rear platform, which would have delayed boarding and largely removed the point of an open rear entrance. With no rear glazing the platform would probably have been rather gloomy.

This very smooth, attractive and radical update of the basic Routemaster shape was submitted by Chris Ashby. It was another to use glazing in areas not normally glazed on buses, reflecting attention being given to the passenger experience as well as the external look.

Associate Editor of *Autocar* magazine Hilton Holloway worked with Rolf Schepp of Lineale Design on this entry for the NBfL competition. The thinking behind the design was to get quite close to the Routemaster, but to give it a much more modernist edge in the same way Land Rover re-invented the Discovery with the Mk3 model. The nose design refers to the classic grille design of the RM, but treats it in a much more minimalist style, pushing it back instead of standing proud. The wrap-around cockpit is also a reference to the RM's half cab. The sloping and heavily glazed front end of the upper deck was partly designed to give the bus a more modern and dynamic feel. A scrolling LED sign in the central band would have shown the bus's route.

There had been a general belief among the designers, right or wrong, that the winner of the competition would see his or her design progressed to produce the finished bus – indeed many of the entrants would not have devoted so much time to it had they thought otherwise. It became clear at the time the prizewinners were announced that no single idea would be used but that all the ideas would be looked at for feeding into the final design, which would be subject to a separate tender process. In Transport Commissioner Peter Hendy's words: 'What we should aim to create now is not just a Routemaster replacement but a whole new generation of London buses that could affect the future of the entire industry'. He went on to say that the process could not be rushed and that the end result might be more radical than anyone had yet proposed.

While the designs – particularly the one involving prestige car maker Aston Martin – attracted considerable interest in the press, there were still some strong dissenting voices. Val Shawcross, the Labour member for transport on the Greater London Assembly, dismissed the whole idea: 'The design competition may have been fun and the winning designs are extremely impressive, but this is not a serious way to make policy and not a worthwhile use of public money. I have yet to hear one convincing argument for why London needs a new double-decker bus and until Boris comes up with some, Londoners will see this as little more than a vanity project.'

There was understandable nervousness about the requirement to have an open platform. This was 2008, not fifty years earlier. In a compensation culture, would TfL be responsible if someone, perhaps under the influence of drink, did not quite manage to hop on the bus and found themselves under the wheels of the vehicle instead? Such nervousness overlooked the fact that deaths of passengers have occurred by their getting trapped in the centre doors of buses.

The concerns were dismissed and Johnson and TfL pressed ahead with developing a bus. The winning entries were passed by TfL to bus manufacturers for them to draw up detailed final designs meeting all relevant legislation, and later presented to TfL for consideration on a competitive-tender basis. In April 2009, a formal invitation to express interest in the project was published in the *Official Journal of the European Union* which is a legal requirement for any tenders above around £200,000. Six bus manufacturers were the following month invited to negotiate for the contract to design and build the new bus: Alexander Dennis, EvoBus (which included Mercedes-Benz buses), Hispano Carrocera, Optare, Scania AB and Wrightbus. In contrast to the competition specifications, the contract called for a bus with a capacity for at least 87 passengers, two staircases, three doors, and an open rear platform able to be closed off when not required, such as at night. The bus would be a hybrid, about 11 metres long, utilising technology to make it 40 per cent more fuel efficient than conventional diesel buses, and 15 per cent more fuel efficient than London hybrid buses already in operation. The winner would have to have the capability of building 600 buses over three years.

Two of the six dropped out quickly: Scania reckoned the timetable for the introduction of the prototype was not feasible, while EvoBus had concerns over its lack of double-decker experience. Then Hispano Carrocera dropped out and, eventually, after Optare announced in November 2009 that it was 'no longer in the running', the list was whittled down to just two: Alexander Dennis and Wrightbus.

The final submissions were received by TfL from the two remaining in the contest on 4th December 2009. Alexander Dennis went to the length of submitting three different three-door body designs: one from the Aston Martin and Foster partnership, one from Capoco Design and one of their own (see pages 23-25) while Wrights submitted just an in-house design. Wrightbus had been seen as an outsider because it was principally a bus body builder, rather than whole bus manufacturer, using chassis from established companies such as Volvo and Scania. A clue may have been provided in a visit by Peter Hendy to Wright's Northern Ireland factory to inspect their forthcoming Gemini 2 hybrid at the beginning of October. He did not take the trouble to visit ADL. The contract for the bus was awarded to Wrightbus on 23rd December 2009.

There was even more surprise the following month when TfL announced that it was Heatherwick Studio (which had not been involved in the original bid) that had been appointed to help Wrightbus produce the final design. The result of the process, therefore, was that the two designs which had won the competition were edged out in the final choice by a bus body building company which required a designer, not involved in the competition or the bidding process, to help produce the bus.

WRIGHTBUS v ALEXANDER DENNIS

STEWART J BROWN

As mentioned in the previous chapter, by the end of 2009 the potential manufacturers of the NBfL had been reduced to two, Alexander Dennis (ADL) and Wrightbus, who between them were already supplying the bulk of the buses used on London routes. They were for a number of reasons the obvious choices, including the scale of their operations and that, as established suppliers of buses to London, they knew not just the decision-makers at TfL, but also the operators who would be running the buses.

A contract for 600 buses of an advanced design for one of the world's great capital cities carries considerable prestige. But when you spread that over three years it equals just four buses a week – four buses to a unique specification unlikely to interest other cities. One of the potential bidders, EvoBus, is part of the Daimler organisation which builds almost 40,000 buses a year. Scania's annual bus production is approaching 9,000 vehicles. No company likes to turn away potentially profitable business, but for global manufacturers the attraction of building one bus a day for one customer must be limited.

The other British builder in the running, Optare, was in 2009 in the throes of reorganisation and it is doubtful if, at that time, it had the resources to handle such a challenging contract as the NBfL.

While both ADL and Wrightbus are significant exporters, they are not global automotive giants. So a 600-vehicle order is significantly more important to their businesses than it would have been to, say, Scania.

ADL had aligned itself with the two first prizewinners in the open competition, Fosters and Capoco, to produce two of its proposals for a complete bus, which would have been based around the company's Enviro400H hybrid double-decker. This used proven components which could have helped cut costs and expedite production. It came as a surprise therefore when Northern Ireland based Wrightbus, with limited experience in chassis manufacture and with few hybrid sales, was selected as the builder of the new bus. ADL's pragmatic approach, developing the NBfL around existing units, was beaten by the willingness of Wrightbus to start with a clean sheet of paper.

Both manufacturers had been supplying buses to London for some 25 years. ADL predecessor Dennis had established itself as a major force in London first with the Dart midibus, supplying large numbers in the 1990s, and then from 1999 with the double-deck Trident. Bodybuilder Alexander won a number of orders in the 1990s, and became a major supplier from the end of the decade with its ALX400 double-deck body for low-floor chassis.

Wright – as the company was then known – started supplying London at the end of the 1980s, with bodies on Renault S75 and Dennis Dart chassis. Where other bodybuilders used conventional aluminium framing for their bodies, Wright chose a system developed by Alusuisse in which a deep aluminium extrusion ran the full length of the bus below the window line and was a key component in the strength of the structure. Wright further developed this to create its Aluminique system with its R3 split pillar in which the bottom section of the body pillar – the area most vulnerable to damage in minor traffic accidents – can be easily removed and replaced, reducing downtime and repair costs.

But apart from its distinctive construction methods, one of the hallmarks of Wright has been its willingness to innovate. The first low-floor buses in London, 68 Dennises and Scanias in 1994, were bodied by Wright, some of which were for Peter Hendy's Centrewest company. Wright been the only UK volume producer of articulated buses, on Volvo and Scania chassis. The first serious trial of artics in London, by First CentreWest in 2001, involved Wright-bodied Volvos. The company was also a pioneer in the exploration of alternative power sources, producing a hybrid single-decker, the Electrocity, with a Capstone microturbine as its power source as long ago as 2001. And it was selected by First to build the impressive articulated StreetCar. According to Hendy's foreword in *The Wright Way*, the story of the company, Wright's had been dismantling an old Routemaster 'to learn the lessons of the past in a bid to be part of the future' while the public competition was going on in 2008.

Yet being a pioneer did not always pay off. When low-floor single-deckers became the London standard, very few were bodied by Wright as operators chose the Dennis Dart SLF, typically with Plaxton bodywork. When articulated buses came to the capital they were built in Germany, not in Northern Ireland. And, as history shows, the microturbine was not the way forward for hybrid drive systems. The Electrocity name was revived in 2006 for a batch of hybrids delivered to Go-Ahead London. These were not a success as their small diesel engines were unable to cope with the demands of intensive bus operation. They were later fitted with Cummins engines while retaining a hybrid drive, and this solved the problem. Wrightbus has also supplied the only hydrogen-fuelled buses currently running in Britain, operated in London by Tower Transit and based on chassis supplied by VDL.

While Wright has been steadily growing over the last two decades, the early 2000s were a difficult period for Alexander and Dennis, which in 2001 were united in common ownership by the Mayflower group and renamed TransBus International. Mayflower collapsed in 2004, and the main part of what had been TransBus International emerged as ADL. TransBus did develop one model aimed at London, the original Enviro200. This – foreshadowing the NBfL – had its Cummins engine in the rear offside corner which made room for an exit door in the rear overhang. One of its most unusual features was the use of larger wheels at the rear than at the front. This permitted the use of Super single tyres at the rear, making room for a wide step-free gangway running the full length of the bus. This version of the Enviro200 got no further than two prototypes. It was a victim of the Mayflower collapse, but was also the wrong bus for the time. London was moving away from single-deckers to double-deckers, and no operator outside the capital wanted a bus with an exit in the rear overhang.

While ADL and its Alexander predecessor has been building double-deckers for 70 years, Wrightbus only started building double-deckers in 2001, its first order being 50 on Volvo B7L chassis for Arriva London. The company has continued to work closely with Volvo in the production of double-deckers, including Volvo's B5LH hybrid. But it started offering its own complete double-decker in 2008, using chassis supplied by VDL. The first hybrid versions, the Gemini 2 HEV, entered service with First in London at the end of that year. For the NBfL Wrightbus is building its own chassis, and in the summer of 2013 commissioned a purpose-built factory to do this. As well as building the NBfL, this factory has the capacity to handle other products, including a new, lighter, double-decker currently under development.

The ADL business which emerged from the failure of Mayflower was revitalised and immediately set about producing a range of new models, including a double-decker with a Dennis-built chassis and an Alexander-built body, the Enviro400. Close co-operation between chassis and body designers helped optimise the internal layout and to maximise the number of seats in the lower saloon. The Enviro400 quickly proved a success in London and elsewhere, both with conventional diesel and hybrid drive trains, the latter being the Enviro400H. And while ADL lost out on the NBfL contract, it continues to be a major supplier of double-deckers to the capital with the Enviro models. Indeed, while the spotlight may understandably be focused on the NBfL, it is important to remember that most of the new buses being delivered to London are still conventional designs from ADL, Volvo and Wrightbus. Today ADL is the UK's biggest bus and coach manufacturer, with 2,300 employees. Wrightbus employs 1,400 people.

ADL is the leading supplier of hybrid buses in the UK, with almost 700 in service. While Wrightbus was the first to deliver hybrids to London, with its Electrocity single-deckers in 2006, ADL was the first with hybrid double-deckers, delivering Enviro400Hs to Go-Ahead and Metroline in 2008. The first Wrightbus hybrids, for Arriva, followed in 2009. London has Europe's biggest fleet of hybrid buses, followed by Manchester and Barcelona.

Outside London, ADL has scored considerable success with Stagecoach, which runs almost 240 Enviro400Hs and a small number of Enviro350H single-deckers. ADL has also supplied Enviro400Hs to, among others, First Glasgow, Lothian Buses, East Yorkshire, Reading Buses, National Express in the West Midlands and Dundee, and Go-Ahead subsidiary Oxford Bus Company. There are no complete Wrightbus hybrids in operation outside London other than StreetCars in Las Vegas.

To set their businesses in a global context, both ADL and Wrightbus have been expanding outside the UK. ADL acquired Australian bus bodybuilder Custom Coaches in 2012. The company also has links with Kiwi Bus in New Zealand and with North American manufacturer New Flyer, both of which sell buses based on the Enviro200. Wrightbus has in 2013 set up new links with manufacturers in India and Europe. In Europe VDL is to sell the Wrightbus StreetLite midibus, while in India Wrightbus is working in association with Daimler to build buses for the local market.

The New Bus for London is undeniably an important vehicle. It has created a tremendous amount of interest. It has boosted employment at Wrightbus. But it is, and looks set to remain, a niche market product. As with the original Routemaster which inspired it, there look set to be few NBfL buyers outside the city for which it was built.

For the manufacturers' competition that followed the public design competition, Alexander Dennis Ltd submitted three sets of proposals; one it had commissioned from Foster + Partners and Aston Martin, illustrated on this page, one from Capoco Design and one set of in-house designs. The Foster design had echoes of its earlier competition entry but stylishly dealt with the new requirement for three sets of doors. The front doors were of fold in type, the centre doors were plug type and the rear platform had a combination of fold in and slide in doors. Like the other ADL submissions, the bus would have been built on a version of the tried and tested Enviro400H chassis.

Capoco Design created this attractive body for ADL, which it called the London Liner,
looking more like a luxury double deck coach than a bus.

In the new specifications laid down for the design, the bus was to have a minimum capacity of 87 made up of 22 seats in the lower saloon, 40 in the upper and a minimum of 25 standees. Two staircases and three doors were specified, with the rear platform being able to be operated in open mode. Special attention was to be given to making the interior as quiet as possible and free of rattles. The design of a new and unique seating moquette would also be required when the contract was awarded. A prototype bus was to be delivered and placed into trial running by spring 2011 with five delivered and ready for service by January 2012 (later amended to the end of April 2012). The in-house design by ADL came in four alternative varieties with minor differences. An attractive vehicle, 11.1 metres long, it and the other ADL offers lost out to TfL's drive for mechanical innovation.

In May 2008, within days of Boris Johnson's election victory, Wright's had decided, with encouragement from TfL, to acquire an old RM to dismantle in order to learn from its structural techniques. It was the start of a process that was to lead to the company being given the contract to manufacture the New Bus for London. For the 2009 manufacturer's competition they produced a competent in-house design, with minor optional variations, but not one that would stand out from other buses on the streets. Under the skin though was a solidly designed body structure of which Wrightbus was so confident they were able to give a 12-year structural warranty. The thick off-white window pillars inside the NBfL and bonded glazing were a Wrights feature, though Heatherwick did not take much from the external appearance when they were brought in. The headlight arrangement survived and the asymmetrical windscreen was further developed.

HEATHERWICK

JAMES WHITING

If Peter Hendy was a major influence in the choice of Wrightbus to build the NBfL, then the deputy chairman of TfL Daniel Moylan was a major player in the appointment of Heatherwick Studio to design the bodywork. Moylan became chairman of the mayor's Design Advisory Panel (mostly concerned with the built environment) in December 2009 and was well aware of the quality of Heatherwick's work, having spoken highly of it whilst a councillor with the Royal Borough of Kensington and Chelsea.

In January 2010, very soon after the contract had been signed with Wrightbus for building the new bus, Heatherwick Studio was selected by TfL to handle the design of the bodywork and interior detailing. The Kings Cross based studio had been formed in 1994 by Thomas Heatherwick and over the past 20 years has achieved a reputation for cutting edge design. Heatherwick, 39 at the time he was appointed, graduated from the Royal College of Art where he studied furniture design. His capacity for original thinking had become apparent while he was a student at Manchester Polytechnic, where he built a full-size and futuristic looking pavilion in the grounds.

Heatherwick chose as his project leader on the new bus Stuart Wood, who had joined the studio in 2001. Stuart's particular expertise is with 3D computer-aided design work and he also has extensive knowledge of manufacturing processes. He was assisted throughout the design process by the studio's Neil Hubbard. Stuart and Neil visited the Wrightbus factory in Northern Ireland to see buses being built. In Neil's words: 'The great thing about the factory is that you kind of have a mock-up at every stage – you see the production line from chassis level, as they fit the components, up to finished bus'.

It was Wrightbus's job to satisfy the engineering and practical aspects, and Heatherwick's job to satisfy the mayor with an 'iconic' appearance for the new bus. Thomas Heatherwick was a good choice for the job, despite (or perhaps because of) his own admission that he 'knew nothing about buses'. This guaranteed fresh thinking and the bus that has resulted certainly stands out as unlike any other bus on London's streets – or streets elsewhere for that matter.

The benefit to Stuart and Neil of the factory visit was shared by Wrightbus. According to David Barnett, the company's Development Engineering Manager, they learnt from the team the approach of starting with a blank sheet of paper and asking 'why' for each different component on the bus. For some of these there was nothing set in legislation; they had just evolved into the company's standard way of doing things whenever they were designing a bus.

The total fees for the design were £427,500, made up of £50,000 for the design principles, £85,000 for the external design, £150,000 for the interior styling and the balance of £142,500 for the studio's prototyping costs, design support during build and monitoring of the bus up to the delivery of the certified prototype.

According to Barnett, the brief the team was given was: 'If you walk out of the TfL offices to the nearest postcard stand you will find a few iconic images on a postcard; a black taxi, a red phone box and a Routemaster bus. Fast forward five years and you will see a black cab, a red phone box and your design as the iconic London transport image'.

The starting point for Heatherwick, as specified by TfL, was the front and rear end treatment. Wrights had worked on the basic structure of the body and had produced its own body design also, but its look was not what Boris Johnson was seeking. Heatherwick's job was to transform it into an iconic design. Early sketches show the front and rear glazing extending to floor level on the nearside, generous curves in the front and rear domes and shallow upper-deck windows. Style was paramount. However, the shallow upper-deck windows also aimed to reduce the effect of the sun on the interior temperature. A stylish flow was given to the front of the bus by wrapping round the front upper deck windows and having the driver's windscreen sweep down from offside to nearside. The beautifully sweeping glazed rear, Heatherwick's favourite part of the bus, invites passengers on to the upper deck and echoes the open-staircase buses of the 1920s.

The unveiling to the press of the computer aided drawings of the exterior design was held at Battersea bus garage on 17th May 2010 at which time the interior was still being finalised. Here, people learned that a full size static mock up was being worked on for completion later in the year. Boris Johnson, who performed the unveiling with Peter Hendy, spoke of the new bus as not only beautiful but also having a 'green heart beating beneath its stylish, swooshing exterior'.

One of a series of TfL computer generated images of the design released to the media in May 2010. At about the same time, work began at the Wrightbus factory on the full size mock-up.

The previous month, TfL was still seeking reassurance from the Department for Transport that the bus, in its planned configuration, would get approval to operate. Conditional reassurance came in an email dated 12th April from the DfT to the project's leader David Hampson-Ghani, following a visit to the Department's offices by the bus's technical consultant Chris Dyal. The DfT's Donald Macdonald wrote to say that they had 'reached a conclusion which gives more confidence about the approval of this vehicle design' (doubts had been expressed earlier). He questioned whether TfL was planning to seek approval at European level and continued: 'While we believe that there is no impediment to the approval of an open platform design with two different modes of operation, the European approach would perhaps result in a greater level of scrutiny by other member states and the European Commission, simply because such approvals have validity throughout the EC'. Further contacts between TfL and the DfT took place on the matter but, as things turned out, there was to be no impediment put in the way of the bus either by the UK licensing authority or by Europe. EC Whole Vehicle Type Approval was later granted.

Originally, it had been planned that the forward staircase would be of similar layout to the Wright Gemini and common to London buses generally; that is with just the bottom step angled towards the centre door. At the request of London Travelwatch, two steps at the foot of the staircase were turned 90 degrees to the higher ones, giving as a by-product a little more floor space. The main reason for the request was to reduce the potential distance someone could fall on the stairs. At one point, according to a contemporary report, the upper deck layout provided for an area free of seating at the top of these stairs, with a double seat on the nearside only at the front. When the mock up was built, the only seat fitted to the bus in the front three-quarters of the upper deck was the one at the front offside so if it was ever planned to omit this, the plan had been superseded by then.

Hector Serrano's second prize-winning design in the competition included the idea of a glazed staircase that was not unlike the one opposite the centre door of the NBfL.

The full size mock up of the NBfL was built at the Ballymena factory and shipped across the Irish Sea, as the buses themselves would be starting a year later. It was constructed using mostly the materials of a real bus for its body shell and placed on a scrap Scania chassis. It could however be moved by low loader only, not towed. The mock up was given the classification MN0123, MN being the initials of Wright's managing director Mark Nodder. The registration letters were reportedly chosen by project leader Hampson-Ghani as of personal significance. It was transported, unsheeted despite an air of secrecy, to the London Transport Museum's Acton depot at the beginning of November 2010 in readiness for it to be shown to the press, TfL bus staff and service contractors and passenger groups for their comments. At a launch on 11th November, attended by Johnson, Peter Hendy and the Secretary of State for Northern Ireland, Owen Paterson, those present got their first view of the bus in life-size form. Boris, clearly delighted with the end result, described the bus as 'delectable' and 'amazing'.

Parked alongside earlier London bus designs from the Museum's collection, the mock up made an impressive sight. The responses from those who visited it at Acton during its period there were mostly positive and almost everyone spoke well of the exterior appearance. Visitors included members of the London Assembly, senior transport officers of the London boroughs, the bus operating companies and unions, London Travelwatch, and a number of groups representing passengers with special needs – mobility groups on behalf of wheelchair users, those concerned with the welfare of people with learning difficulties, and the Royal National Institutes for the Blind and the Deaf. The interior made extensive use of plywood and a maximum of four people were permitted upstairs.

The mock up gave those who saw it their first look at the interior of the bus. There were echoes of the Routemaster in the double bench seating (but with separate sets of cushions for each seated passenger), the colouring of the seat fabric and walls and in the Treadmaster cork-resin flooring used on the front and rear platforms.

Overleaf The mock up was exhibited alongside earlier London buses from the LT Museum collection.

RCL 2229

RF 537

world
itement.

Opposite and left
Between the display of the mock up and the building of the prototypes, a few other changes were made, including handrails being added to the raised seats in the lower deck, a 'next stop' electronic display added to the nearside rear bulkhead for the benefit of passengers in the rear facing seats and the seat edges finished in a striped moquette pattern rather than plain red. The brackets that can be seen on the window pillars just forward of the raised seating were for the fitting of bracing during the mock ups transit. Four different moquette patterns are used on the NBfL, three of which are variations on the same theme: one for the seat cushions and two for the different heights of seat back. The fourth uses the same colours but is a plain pattern of solid rectangles used for the sides of the seat cushions (though not on the mock up) and the wheelchair area. Up to the time the mock up was built, the 'Buses' roundel had not appeared on buses.

Groups representing wheelchair users had the most comments in terms of possible alterations and there was some pressure for the new bus to have two wheelchair spaces to allow for the fact that wheelchair users sometimes like to travel with friends who are also wheelchair-bound. It was pointed out that not only was it necessary to balance the needs of all users but that a second wheelchair space was not possible because there was insufficient flat floor area available. Only one change was made to the mock up while at Acton; the pole between the wheelchair bay and the centre door was modified in January 2011 to improve accessibility. It was also agreed that an additional horizontal handrail half way up the front staircase would be fitted to the buses when built and that the gold-coloured handrails would be slightly more yellow to assist the visually impaired.

The upper deck was mostly empty of seating; there was one pair of seats in front of the forward staircase and five pairs at the back. The rest was an empty floor. A major criticism was about the height of the ceiling upstairs. Of a sample of 127 people questioned, 46% said it was a little too low and 19% much too low. The ceiling was indeed lower above the seats (but not in the aisle) and the effect was probably exaggerated to some extent by the fact that there was no natural light entering the mock up and the artificial light that was provided could make it feel quite claustrophobic.

Seat spacing took quite a lot of thought, Heatherwick aiming to give as many passengers as possible a good view through the windows. This aim has been achieved more successfully on the upper deck than downstairs, where the scope for avoiding thick window pillars in the line of view was much more limited, the seat positions being dictated by the door positions, the axles and the wheelchair space. The least satisfactory seat is perhaps the rear-facing offside one on the lower deck where the forward view is of the blank wall between the saloon and the engine compartment. There are no forward facing passenger seats ahead of the centre door and only six altogether downstairs compared to ten facing the back. Again this is unavoidable in view of the chassis layout. Some have commented that more headroom, and less of a step up to the seats, at the rear of the lower deck would have been achieved by having inward facing bench seats (as on the RM and some of the competition entries). However, the width of the wheelarches prevented this, the offside one including the drive to the generator.

Opposite The upper deck of the mock up, devoid of most of the seating and without the distinctive lighting, did not look particularly inviting. Only the rear section was complete in its furnishing.

The forward stairs of the mock up. The Oyster card reader at the foot of the stairs was moved when the prototypes were built and the handrail on the right in the second photograph made shallower.

After four months at Acton, the mock up was moved to the Museum's main Covent Garden site in March where it could be seen by a wider public. It was on display there until the end of November when it was moved for storage, and possible use of body parts, to London General's Mandela Way East garage.

When the prototypes appeared there was very little difference between them and the mock up, the exact provision and positioning of handrails being one of the minor changes. In the finished buses, though, it was possible to appreciate fully the styling and how it feels to the passenger. The interior colour scheme's more traditional feel, using burgundy and soft white, has been well received. The burgundy was used for the lower half of the walls and as the base colour for the seats, so that the bus would 'look good dirty'. 'If it's a slushy, winter day,' explained Heatherwick, 'and seventy schoolkids get on, the floor is going to get covered in salty slush, and the seats might have a bit of kebab or whatever.' Specific comments from people who had inspected the mock up varied from 'Stylish patterning' and 'Appealing retro look' to 'Colours unappealing' and 'Too old fashioned'. Overall, about three-quarters of those questioned liked the seat fabric colour and design.

Lighting is also a break away from modern trends in bus design. Although the first computer-generated illustrations produced by TfL, those issued to the press in May 2010, included one night-time impression with the interior lit by fluorescent tubes, this form of lighting was never intended. Fluorescent lighting, said Heatherwick, was the least flattering form of light to human tissue: 'It's what you have on a battery chicken farm'. So it was shunned in favour of circular LED lights placed at intervals along the ceilings. These create a more restful environment after dark than bright fluorescent tubes.

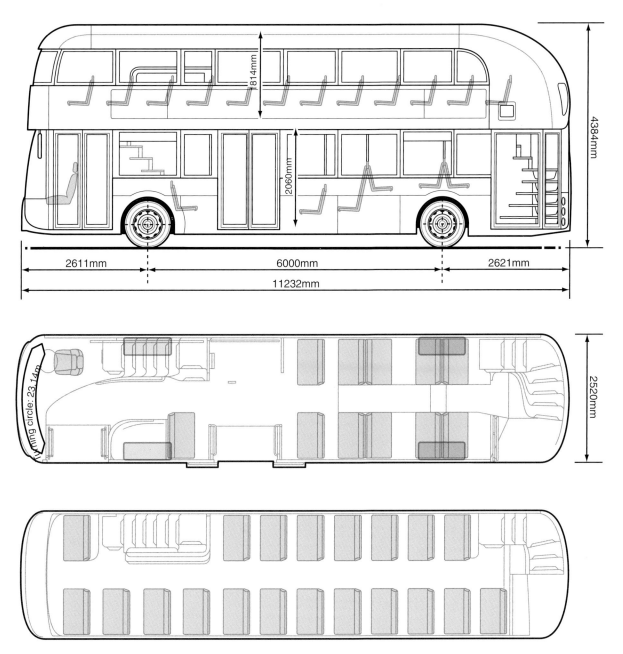

The decision to have non-opening windows that was to cause problems when the bus entered service was not left to Heatherwick; indeed in an interview for the *Daily Telegraph* in June 2011 he lamented: 'Buildings used to have windows that opened, trains used to have windows that opened, but now more and more things are sealed and enclosed'. At the launch of the first prototype at the end of that year, the press were told that no decision had been made on whether the production vehicles would have opening windows, so the performance of the cooling system on the prototypes was intended to inform this decision. However the plain windows certainly contribute to the sleek appearance of the bus, and opening windows upstairs would interfere with the passenger's view in a way that other modern double-deckers with their taller windows do not. The main reason non-openers were decided on however was to avoid interference with the air cooling system.

The finished dimensions of the bus and the seating layouts downstairs and upstairs. These drawings show well why it was necessary to employ a slightly greater than ideal length for the new bus if capacity was not to be compromised. All space available for seating is used and a length more normal on London double deckers of 10.6m would have given eight fewer seats.

The styling upstairs is somewhat different from that downstairs. On the upper deck, in common with the designers of the Virgin Pendolino trains, Heatherwick went for an aircraft feel. The lower deck interior, with many more constraints on the layout and design, is more workmanlike and functional, though the ceiling, window frames and seats follow the same style. The rear end is very distinctive, not least because of the diagonal glazing that extends to the upper deck. Despite the presence of the engine compartment under the stairs there is a shallow set-back area that was also a feature in the Routemaster design as a place for the conductor to stand out of the way of passengers boarding or alighting. In practice this has proved to be a very warm place for the conductor to stand; welcome perhaps in the winter months.

The gold-coloured stanchions, which smoothly incorporate the wireless bell pushes, are a nice touch, as also are the burgundy-coloured Oyster card readers. Heatherwick had originally hoped that faux leather could be used for these, but this material was not considered the most practical, an example of the small compromises that had to be accepted.

Attention to detail: a ceiling light, seat rail, burgundy Oyster card reader, wireless bell push integrated into a pole, and top of staircase.

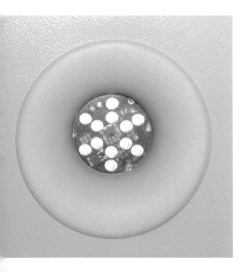

A scale model of the rear section of the NBfL as exhibited at a special Heatherwick exhibition at the Victoria & Albert Museum in the summer of 2012.

Another small compromise was in the front upper deck window corner pillars. Passengers sitting by the side windows at the front find themselves looking straight ahead at a thick white pillar. This pillar was originally designed by Heatherwick to have been much thinner (see photo of the mock up of the upper deck on page 35). It was also a matter of some regret to the designers that so many vinyl stickers were needed. The utilitarian driver's mirrors half way along the lower deck interior (for the wheelchair space and the centre door) are other essential add-ons not designed by Heatherwick that detract to some extent from the overall appearance.

The seats may perhaps benefit from Heatherwick's studies in furniture design when he was at the RCA. The seat covering is a pleasing return to the colours used originally in the Routemaster but the pattern is very different. 'In the seat pattern,' says Heatherwick in an interview, 'we designed a repeat that was as big as the body. The distortion pattern is the same shape as your body, like contours of it.' In an interview for an exhibition held at the V&A between 31st May and 30th September 2012, Heatherwick gave some further details of their aims: 'The brief was never to remake something from the past, but we have not tried to reinvent ideas that don't need reinventing if there are things in the past that are useful. One of the most basic of these was the bus seats. At the moment when you get into a bus your eyes are bombarded with all these plastic bucket seats, and each one has a handle at the top of the seat and a crevice that a crisp packet can get caught in. We have reintroduced the bench seat with just one handrail across the top. All buses used to have that.' Two weeks after the V&A exhibition of the studio's work opened, Thomas Heatherwick spoke on Radio 4's *Today* programme: 'Dignity sounds quite a pompous word, but we were thinking about how we could reintroduce some of that feeling of the magic of travelling in a bus'. The studio seems to have succeeded.

MILLBROOK

HILTON HOLLOWAY

20th June 2011 was a day that the political opponents of London Mayor Boris Johnson had convinced themselves would never arrive. But on an overcast morning in Bedfordshire, I was one of a gathering of journalists at the giant Millbrook test track to view the first prototype of the 'New Bus for London' emerging from the distance. Johnson, standing on the vehicle's open platform, was understandably extra-bullish as the bus pulled up in the front of the assembled media. I was also rather wide-eyed because – as mentioned earlier in this book – I had visited Johnson in his campaign office in the old GLC building, back in early December 2007 with just such a proposal for a 'New Routemaster'. And here it was, a New Bus For London in its final form and, as we later saw, just a year away from entering service trials on the capital's streets.

To understand why Johnson's one-vehicle victory parade in Bedfordshire was such an important moment for him – after all this was a prototype of a new bus not an attempt to put a man on Mars – it is necessary to remember how extraordinarily political his New Routemaster policy had been from the moment Johnson declared that he wanted to see a 'modern day' version of the Routemaster bus introduced to London.

I was fascinated by the Routemaster's structural integrity and refinement, compared to much newer buses. At worst, conventional rear-engined double-decker buses of the time seemed to be shaking themselves to pieces when idling, passengers being rattled by the big diesel engine seemingly trying to leap off its mounts. To me, these buses were also particularly noisy and unrefined, especially when pulling away from standstill. There seemed to be a serious lack of attention to what the car industry calls Noise, Vibration and Harshness. Recent bus designs have addressed this, but the NBfL goes further. Later, TfL boss Peter Hendy told me that the Routemaster's riveted aluminium monocoque structure was probably based on what the London Transport workshops had learnt from building Halifax bomber fuselages in World War 2. Perhaps it shouldn't have been a surprise that the Routemaster lasted so much longer on a London duty cycle that wore out more modern buses.

By a very handy coincidence Johnson's vision of an open platform was the perfect opening for adopting a non-mainstream hybrid transmission and one that is arguably more robust and easily repairable over the long term. This transmission uses electric motors to drive the rear wheels and the engine is used a generator, feeding the electric motors and trickle charging the on-board battery, which accelerates the bus away from standstill without generating any pollution.

Explaining to the wider world why the NBfL was so different mechanically to nearly every other vehicle is very difficult. Although the production version is labelled as a 'hybrid' – something most people recognise from automotive world – the bus is actually driven purely by electricity. The rear wheels are driven by

Opposite The test rig at Millbrook on 20th June 2011, when on display to the press. The rear offside corner panel covering the engine compartment is in fibreglass on the buses built for service.

electric motors, which are powered by both the bus's onboard battery pack and by a relatively small diesel engine (at just 4.5-litres in size, it is only twice the size of the diesel engine in the Range Rover Evoque). The diesel engine drives a generator, providing electricity for wheel motors.

The key difference between the NBfL's drive train and that used by conventional hybrids is that the NBfL's engine is not mechanically connected to the wheels, using only high-tension cables to transmit the electricity to the wheel motors. This set-up is known as a 'series hybrid' as opposed to the parallel hybrids, which have an electric motor sandwiched between the engine and gearbox. Arguably, the NBfL's arrangement has two crucial advantages for a hard-worked public service vehicle: first it is much less complex than a conventional hybrid. Secondly, this system uses a single gear ratio, the lack of gear changing making the ride smoother for passenger. Also, like the original Routemaster, the engine/generator can be removed relatively easily for replacement or repair.

Conventional buses have to have a rear-mounted engine, in order for the bus floor to be set low for easy access. In the original Routemaster, which had the engine at the front, the floor had to be raised high in order to clear the propshaft that ran under the bus, taking power to the rear wheels. With the series transmission, the engine/generator package could be neatly fitted in one corner (in this case, under the stairs), connected to the rear motors by heavy-duty cables, leaving the whole rear end of the bus open for the installation of a rear staircase and open rear platform.

Opposite The NBfL Development Vehicle, or test rig, was never intended to become a completed bus for passenger service. It was built solely for putting the design to the range of tests needed. Its front door is single leaf and hinged. It has no centre doors, just a fitment to give an impression of them. Being unpainted, it showed the three different materials used for the exterior bodywork: aluminium, fibreglass (white) and Wright's composite material (maroon).

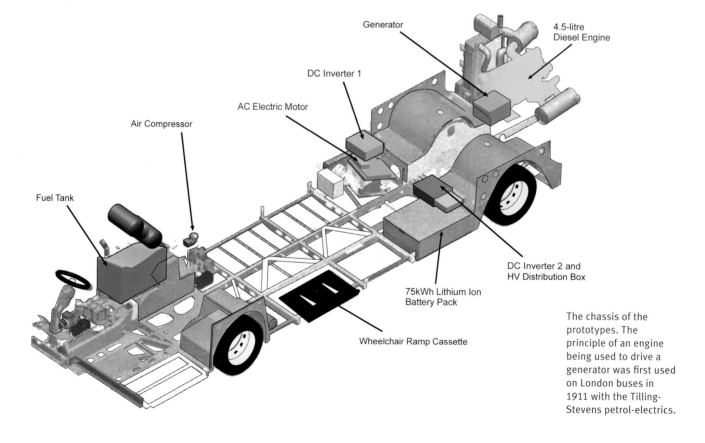

The chassis of the prototypes. The principle of an engine being used to drive a generator was first used on London buses in 1911 with the Tilling-Stevens petrol-electrics.

During the two years of development, the arguments about whether Mayor Johnson should be pursuing his policy of a bespoke bus for London continued to rage. Much of the, often deeply hostile, exchanges took place on the internet, particularly in the *Guardian*'s 'London Blog'. And many of the accusations were remarkably ill informed, such as the oft-repeated proposition that spending £11m on five (later eight) prototypes and the research and development needed for an entirely new kind of bus was a 'waste of money'.

Ask anybody in the car industry what an £11m investment would achieve, and the answer would probably be not much more than a set of new headlights and tail lamps. In stark contrast came the retorts that Transport for London, under Ken Livingstone, had spent £94m installing two lifts at Green Park tube station. Certainly, Britain's media and political elite are not over-endowed with engineers.

With his trademark overstatement, Johnson addressed the press pack at Millbrook and referred to the prototype's bare patchwork aluminium finish, comparing its appearance to that of the 1936 Supermarine Spitfire prototype. Despite appealing for recognition of the comparison from the assembled hacks, none came. I was probably the only other person at Millbrook who had seen the same pictures of the Spitfire prototype. Such knowledge of Britain's engineering achievements used to be a schoolboy staple.

As well as Johnson driving the bus for a short distance on the Millbrook apron, journalists were also allowed to experience a very short ride on the bus, again underlining that Johnson's vision had become reality. For those of an engineering bent, this prototype was especially fascinating because, for probably the first and last time, the guts of the New Bus for London were exposed.

Wrightbus's own aluminium spaceframe construction (a clever and efficient mix of simple aluminium extrusions and bolt-together joints) was on display inside the bus, as were the on-board electronic sensors, which were measuring every tiny deflection in the structure as this prototype was subjected to the Millbrook test regime.

Upper deck front and rear views showing measuring equipment installed in the test rig and Wright's Aluminique construction.

Although it wasn't readily apparent to the visiting press, the Millbrook test facility is enormous, taking in more than the high-speed bowl. Millbrook, among the many specific test areas, has three demanding Alpine-like hill routes, which are used to test braking, handling and transmissions. It also has a track course designed to simulate city driving and various rough and specially moulded road surfaces to check the amount of noise, vibration and harshness that is being transmitted into a vehicle.

'Twist humps' (a series of angled humps moulded into a tarmac roadway) are used to test the structural integrity of a vehicle. Finally, Millbrook also carries out the famous 'tilt test' where a bus is put on a tilting platform to ensure it can lean at precipitous angles before it will actually roll over. The NBfL prototype was put through all of these tests before the first five prototypes were released.

Perhaps most intriguing is Millbrook's all-important 'Drive Cycle' economy and emissions test. Developed by Millbrook and Transport for London, it is based on data from the real world 159 route, which runs from Marble Arch to Streatham Hill via Oxford Street. According to the detailed emissions testing information, the NBfL is the most economical 'Hybrid', beating the Wright's Gemini 2H by 11.6mpg to 10.2mpg. More importantly, in these tests the NBfL had the lowest Nitrogen Oxide and Hydrocarbon emissions of all its rivals.

Although my trip on the prototype was very brief indeed, most satisfying was the smoothness and relative silence of the electric drive train, as well as the promise of greater refinement promised by the unique construction technique. Standing on the deck at the test track, it was clear that this bus had the potential to lead the way in terms of air and noise pollution. And, from a purely selfish point of view, it had the promise to attract cosseted car drivers like me to public transport.

I also came down firmly on the side of Johnson's libertarian approach: much better the carrot of slick, modern, public transport than Livingstone's stick of tolls and road space reduction.

Millbrook Emissions Testing								
Vehicle	System	Euro	HC (g/km)	CO (g/km)	NOx (g/km)	Pm (g/km)	CO2 (g/km)	MPG
Diesels								
Scania	Diesel EGR	E4	0.049	0.090	11.546	0.130	1572.1	4.8
Wright Gemini 2	Diesel SCR	E5	0.028	1.985	7.734	0.053	1250.6	6.0
ADL Enviro400	Diesel SCR	E4	0.051	1.620	8.646	0.045	1253.1	5.9
Volvo B9TL / ADL	Diesel SCR	E4	0.000	0.013	8.583	0.030	1670.3	4.5
Hybrids								
New Bus for London	Siemens Series	E5	0.000	0.11	3.960	0.053	640.2	11.6
Wright Gemini 1H	Siemens Series	E4	0.012	0.039	7.616	0.060	866.0	8.6
Wright Gemini 2H	Siemens Series	E4	0.044	0.115	5.248	0.097	734.4	10.2
ADL Enviro400H	BAE Series	E4	0.053	0.815	8.792	0.029	856.1	8.7
Volvo	ISAM	E5 and EEV	0.020	0.152	6.738	0.043	937.3	8.0

THE LAUNCH AT WRIGHTBUS

GAVIN BOOTH

Launching a new bus to the media normally follows an established format – a gathering of the usual hacks from the trade press, a welcome from the managing director, a PowerPoint presentation by the sales director and then a chance to see, photograph, crawl over and even drive the new product.

The November 2011 launch of NBfL at the Wrightbus Ballymena plant was clearly going to be different. Normally the grapevine means that we have a pretty good idea what we're going to see, but not in the case of NBfL, and it was inevitable that there would be a much wider interest than normal in the new bus and so there were representatives from serious daily newspapers, radio and television stations, in addition to the familiar faces of the transport press.

One of the eight NBfL prototypes under construction at Wrightbus, Ballymena on the day of the November 2011 launch. From this angle, at this stage of construction, it does not look too different from conventional double-deckers.

There was a fair amount of stage management – and why not, after all this would be our first proper glimpse of a bus that had been talked about for some time, even by people who would not normally be interested in buses, and that had received more than its fair share of media coverage even before anybody had actually seen the real thing. And of course there was the Boris factor. We knew that London mayor, Boris Johnson, was going to launch the bus and we all knew that any event involving Boris would never be run of the mill.

At the appointed time the assembled hacks were ushered into the assembly shop where several more NBfLs were under construction, and while that gave us a clue about the shape and style of the bus we were about to see, they were still very much in the early stages of build.

After a wait, the roller shutters on an outside door started to rise and we got our first glimpse of NBfL as it was driven into the shop. This, it was immediately clear, was a bus like no other. I can't recall if it got a round of applause but perhaps it should have done. What we were seeing had redefined the look of double-deck buses at a stroke, and its combination of bold styling with more than a nod to the past certainly ticked all the boxes.

From the rear the individual look of NBfL becomes clearer during construction, with the rounded rear dome in position and the aperture for the rear entrance very much in evidence. The composite rear end combines strength and weight saving. Any car that runs into the back of the bus is guaranteed to come off worse.

47

On the back platform was Boris Johnson, for the mainstream media possibly as much a star as the bus itself. He jumped off the platform to address the assembled crowd of local politicians, the Wrightbus staff who had worked on the development of the bus, TfL hierarchy and of course the media representing newspapers, magazines, radio and television.

'We've got this fantastic new bus,' he said, 'on which, amidst many other features, we've got the open platform back. We're going to bring that back to the streets of London – it was wrongly taken away. This is a world-class piece of technology built here in Ballymena. It's the most amazing futuristic design, but it's also the cleanest, greenest bus that will ply the streets of London, indeed any city in the UK.'

Johnson fielded the media questions as only he can – wittily but clearly demonstrating a knowledge of and commitment to the whole project. He spoke passionately about the bus, hailing it as a revolution in taste and design, and a great investment in London and British technology. 'The design will go round the world,' he said, 'influencing buses in London and elsewhere.' He continued: 'It's not just a bus, it's a visible statement of confidence in tough times and a reminder of TfL's role in driving jobs and investment throughout the UK.' He even referred back to the influence of Frank Pick in prewar London Transport, and Pick's statement that 'every bus should be a piece of street furniture', a view shared by Heatherwick Studio, which described the bus as 'moving architecture'. And Boris couldn't resist a dig at bendy buses 'threatening cyclists and belching out smoke like wounded bull elephants'. Then it was a chance to look inside to discover the

The wait is over as guests get their first glimpse of the NBfL at the Ballymena launch. Although a mock-up had been on view at the London Transport Museum, this was a first chance to see the real thing.

innovative interior design, again a fusion of what seemed to be traditional ideas with modern materials and design concepts. After that we were ushered outside to witness the sight of Boris Johnson driving the new bus out of the assembly shop into the November sunshine.

At the time there was great speculation about the long-term prospects of NBfL. Would there ever be more than eight, we wondered. In conversation, Leon Daniels, TfL's Managing Director – Surface Transport, was being cagey, saying that as 'an old-fashioned bus person it is my view that the next job is to get thousands of miles on this prototype fleet before we take any further decisions on what happens next, because in the history of London buses over the last 100 years the ones that have been rigorously tested before going into production have lasted 50 years and represented very, very good value for the taxpayer and the ones that were rushed into production lasted five minutes and cost a huge amount of money'.

Leon's caution was understandable, and of course we know now that there will be at least 608 of them. It may not achieve the sales outside London that Boris was anticipating, at least not in London three-door form, but it looked to be well suited to London's needs, especially as the unit price of £330,000 that was being suggested at the 2011 launch has proved to be not too wide of the mark, and not significantly more than the cost of some high-spec hybrid double-deckers already in service in the UK. After the assembled media had finished with Boris Johnson he was whisked away to allow those of us who were left to explore the bus in more detail and to give Leon Daniels the chance he had probably been waiting for all day – a quick drive of the bus that TfL had financed.

The bus being slowly driven out into the sunshine, with Boris Johnson at the wheel.

THE LAUNCH IN LONDON

JAMES WHITING

After its launch at Ballymena on 4th November 2011, the first New Bus for London spent some further time at the factory and was shipped over to England on 12th December ready for its London launch on the 16th. It arrived at Ash Grove garage on the 13th and on the following day it had its special exterior adverts and safety notices fitted and the Ibus vehicle location system commissioned. The 15th was set aside for training the driving instructors who would in turn be training the Ash Grove drivers selected to work on the bus when it entered passenger service.

The bus was carrying its newly selected classification of LT (a bow to London Transport) which had been decided on after the Ballymena launch. It replaced the even more prosaic HWP (Hybrid Wright Platform) that had previously been spoken of. It also carried a new registration number – L61AHT to L61HHT having been allocated to LTs 1–8. Although there had been some talk of a public competition to find a name for the bus, a decision had been taken by now not to name it. This had not stopped quite a lot of names being suggested, many if not most ending with 'master'.

The big day was Friday 16th December. LT1 arrived at City Hall about 5.30am ready to be set up for a live LBC radio broadcast from 7am until 10. It was not the first time a bus had parked outside City Hall but it was not a common occurrence as the area around the GLA's head-quarters is reserved for pedestrians and essential trade vehicles. The bus entered and left the area via Weavers Lane, which varies in width between 3.1 and 3.7 metres; special care was needed therefore and a couple of bollards had to be temporarily removed. LBC's live breakfast show was broadcast from the bus with an interview being included with Boris Johnson between 9.30 and 10, at the end of which LBC's engineers were given 15 minutes to remove all the broadcast equipment. And then Boris, keen to get behind the wheel again, drove the bus a short distance alongside City Hall until Leon Daniels took over the driving via Tooley Street and Stamford Street to Westminster Bridge for a photo shoot. From here Peter Hendy drove the bus to Trafalgar Square, the bus arriving for its launch about 11.15 with Boris on the platform.

With press photographers, and a few members of the public in the right place at the right time, taking their pictures, Boris Johnson waves from the platform of LT1, and shakes hands with an admirer, as it arrives at Trafalgar Square on 16th December.

Apart from the assembled press, the event also attracted passers-by intrigued by the new bus. Boris had been planning to make a speech from the rear platform, but got into the driver's seat again. After answering a few reporters' questions in the driver's seat he moved to the front platform. Here he gave his speech, which varied quite a lot from the speaking notes provided by his press office, showing again how very much he enjoys speaking off the cuff:

'Christmas has come early in the form of this revolutionary new bus whose gleaming coat of red paint and sinuous curves will brighten the day of all who see it humming along our great city's streets. It is the latest, greatest masterpiece of British engineering and design, and I am certain it will become a much loved and iconic vehicle akin to the legendary Routemaster from which it draws so much inspiration.

'It is, of course, complete coincidence that the first one runs past my house. It is a bus designed here in London, styled here in London, built in Britain. The bus has the domed look of the capital – St Paul's, a taxi, a bowler hat.' Referring to the Mercedes articulated buses that had been almost eliminated from London bus routes at the time of this launch he continued: 'Do bendy bus lovers want a British bus that is cleaner, greener, or a German-made bus unsuitable for British streets? I believe the approach we have taken will be copied. This is not a hop-on, hop-off you Frogs, two fingers to Europe, just a simple commonsensical approach to London's needs.'

Further opportunities for press interviews with Boris and with Peter Hendy then followed. The event was also shown on the lunch time news of both BBC television and ITV plus at least one overseas television channel. The bus remained on Trafalgar Square until after sunset so that more members of the public could have the opportunity to inspect it. It was incorrectly reported by the press at the time that the bus had a weight of 11,990kg, which was indeed close to the target weight (the mock up had displayed 11,800kg). LT1 and the rest of the prototypes actually weighed 12,650kg which was to have implications for the number of passengers that could legally be carried. The intended capacity of 87 was reduced to 78 in consequence when the buses entered service.

The moquette on LT1 was manufactured by Camira Fabrics in Austria, but this was deemed 'not to specification' by TfL and production was moved to the company's mill near Huddersfield. This increased the number of items on the bus that were made in the UK. The hybrid control system, electric motors and drive axle come from Germany, the doors from the Netherlands, curved glass from Italy and parts of the main flooring from France. The battery storage system is the only part to come from outside Europe; this is imported from China – a world leader in such systems.

Three key players in the NBfL story: Thomas Heatherwick, TfL Transport Commissioner Peter Hendy and London Surface Transport MD Leon Daniels.

Press and passers-by take a look at the new bus while parked on Trafalgar Square.

The day after the launch at Trafalgar Square, the bus was taken from Ash Grove garage to Stratford to be shown to shoppers visiting the recently opened Westfield shopping development, within sight of the new Olympic Park built for the following year's Olympic Games. As the bus was not allowed into the shopping centre, it was parked rather out of sight on Westfield Avenue, at the time a little used road, so many visitors to Stratford that day would have been unaware of its presence. On the 18th, the Sunday before Christmas, it went to Westfield White City and had a much more prominent position between Shepherd's Bush Underground station and the southern entrance to the shopping development. Here it attracted much interest and there was a high level of awareness among those who boarded it that it was 'Boris's Bus'. The majority of comments were favourable, as appears to have been the case wherever it was shown off, a common question being about when the buses were coming to the enquirer's route.

Its next public display was on 4th January when it visited Bexleyheath Broadway in the morning and Bromley High Street in the afternoon. This was followed by trips to Romford High Street and Ilford High Road on the 5th, Ealing Haven Green and Golders Green station bus layby on the 6th and Sutton High Street and Kingston Town Hall on the 7th.

The local newspaper for Golders Green reported that around 500 people had visited the bus during its stint there on the afternoon of the 6th. Students from a school in Harrow took a trip to the station to see it and a group of American tourists also took an interest. Finchley and Golders Green MP Mike Freer said the bus 'was sure to be a hit,' adding that he thought 'the new bus was excellent, modern, but with a clear echo of the original Routemaster'.

LT1 spent at least part of the next couple of weeks at Millbrook but was back in London for a 'preview ride' on the 23rd. *Telegraph* reporter Andrew Gilligan, later to become the mayor's cycling commissioner, gave the bus a mixed review: 'Although the buses will have conductors for most of the day, the conductor's role has deliberately been made close to pointless ... All this feels like TfL's sneaky bureaucracy (which never really wanted the bus) in action. By giving the conductors no real work to do, TfL is setting them up to be axed at the earliest possible moment ... Boris should put a stop to this transparent ploy. The conductors should sell tickets and swipe Oyster cards at people's seats.' He felt that the three doors led the buses open to bendy bus levels of fare evasion and that the conductors checking fares would pay for themselves in the revenue gained. This may or may not be the case, but the extra revenue would certainly go some way towards the cost and the other benefits of having a second staff member could certainly be argued as justifying the rest of the cost. Gilligan went on to say that he felt most people would love it. Comments from passers-by he spoke to included 'sleek', 'forward-looking' and 'classy'. 'Right down to its chunky bell pushes', he concluded his review, 'the Borismaster is thrillingly evocative of an age when form and function mattered in the public sector, when things were designed to please, to work, and to last.'

It had been announced that LT1 would enter service along with LT2 in February. In the event it was not until 2nd April that the bus was available for service and it was allocated to the 38 until 21st November 2012.

The weekend following the Friday launch at Trafalgar Square saw LT1 being shown off to shoppers at the large Westfield shopping centres at Stratford and White City, the latter being illustrated. Then early in the new year the bus spent four days touring suburban shopping centres such as Kingston, where it is seen generating quite a lot of interest.

The launch and subsequent displays in London of LT1 enabled a closer look at the details that contributed to the bus's overall good looks. Above can be seen the recess under the stairs for the conductor. Frontal details are shown opposite.

Overleaf Views of the very stylish upper deck.

ROAD TEST

MATT PRIOR

Public bodies have a tendency – understandably so, given that they're spending our money – to commission products on very specific and objective sets of factors. A jet fighter, for example, is measured by its ability to blow up other jet fighters; road signs are chosen for their clarity, not their beauty. Public procurement cares little for sentimentality. Here, however, is something different. Think of the NBfL – achingly in need of a new name, don't you think? – as more like Heathrow's state-of-the-art Terminal 5 rather than the (barely) functional Terminal 3. NBfL's creators, Northern Ireland bus builder Wrightbus and design studio Heatherwick, have created a new London bus with a product that's almost as much about design flair as it is about transport. Almost. There's only so much you can do with a bus, after all.

Underneath its London Transport red skin lie the innovative bones of a novel product. The NBfL has a Wrightbus steel backbone chassis, to which is attached an aluminium superstructure and body. At 11.2m, the NBfL is a long bus, its length augmented by a composite rear section incorporating the rear stairwell. This also covers the generator (the NBfL is a series hybrid, more on which later) and, crucially, acts like a stiffener for the whole shebang.

If a supercar is dominated – and judged – by its engine, and a sports car by its handling, then a bus is absolutely defined by its interior. And nowhere on NBfL is the introduction of surprise and delight – so often a feature in today's cars but conspicuous by its absence in contemporary public transport – more prominent than inside. I don't think it's particularly controversial to suggest that, in general, bus interiors are ugly. It is cheap to fit a squared-off, plain rooflining and strip lights. It maximises interior space, too, but it looks desperately uninviting. By comparison, the NBfL is a triumph of interior design flair. The upper deck's ceiling has the gentle curve of a classic airliner's cabin, while LED soft-light pods casts a warmer, cosier glow than fluorescent tubes could ever hope to illuminate (yet are placed at each row to provide sufficient reading light).

If you've ever seen an urban double decker tottering along a motorway, you'll know that 'performance' doesn't mean the same thing to bus operators as it does to you and me. We didn't have time to strap our VBox timing gear to the NBfL during our test drive, but putting foot flat to floor at Nutts Corner circuit, near Wrightbus's Ballymena factory, revealed that NBfL is capable of making only sedate, albeit sustained and linear, progress. Step-off from rest is decent enough; the 4.5-litre Cummins turbodiesel generator provides power to an air compressor (for the brakes and steering), a 75kWh battery and the Siemens electric motor, which lies beneath a raised seating area at the rear, from where it drives the back axle.

Left The driver's seat is wide and flat, with great forward visibility.

In December 2011, to coincide with the launch of the new bus in London, *Autocar* magazine published a road test of LT1. This chapter is an edited version of that article. Matt Prior is at the wheel in this photo on the Nutts Corner circuit near Wrightbus's Ballymena factory.

It looks like there's quite a lot of lean, doesn't it? There isn't, not really. Or at least it doesn't feel like it from the driver's seat (upper-deck passengers might think differently). Thanks to a big overhang, you're aware that you're sitting way out in front, so it feels slightly precarious and you wouldn't barrel into a corner knowing you're among the first points of contact with anything coming the other way. But the bus steers moderately well and changes of direction are fuss-free. Will it drift? I imagine it would if it were on a frozen lake, but on a damp karting circuit in Northern Ireland I wasn't inclined to find out.

The electric motor does all the driving; the diesel generator is tuned to sit at optimum revs and provide all the power the batteries need, and it runs only when those batteries need topping up (which was most of the time during our test, although regenerative braking will assist on a proper bus route). The generator is overly grumbly during stop-start at the moment, but Wrightbus engineers are working on a fix. Braking is both by the drive motor and pneumatically assisted discs all round; retardation is fine and there's ABS, but pulling the NBfL to a rapid stop, perched as you are in front of, and mostly below, so much metal, isn't the most enjoyable thing you'll ever do in your life.

Here, then, is where we get to the nub of the *Autocar* road test: what's she like to drive? Seated in the widely adjustable but pretty flat driver's seat, you get a supremely clear view forward. The low-set steering wheel is very adjustable, so finding a comfortable driving position is a cinch, but the upright stance and wide chair mean it's more like sitting at a desk than in a car. The pedals are on the flat floor and the wheel is barely off the horizontal. Still, foot on the long-travel brake pedal, handbrake off and, as you ease off the pedal, the NBfL creeps forward with eerie smoothness. Never before has a hybrid drive train seemed so suited to a vehicle.

Fewer buttons are involved in driving the NBfL compared with other buses. The gear selector is the row of three buttons above the handbrake lever. The status of the bus is displayed on a digital panel in front of the driver (top right of the area within the steering wheel, enlarged in the picture below). This includes displays showing open doors, engine revs and the gear selected. Some modifications were made when the production vehicles were built.

It's hard to gauge the ride across what amounts to a big kart track, but where the NBfL did meet imperfections, it ironed them out pretty admirably. On the road we'd expect the largely comfortable float you get in most buses, but with less of the accompanying crash over bigger potholes thanks to the composite rear end's body-stiffening properties. At 2.5 metres across, the NBfL takes up its share of road space, but its turning circle is superb at little more than twice the bus's length.

Nonetheless, if you haven't driven a cab-forward piece of kit before, it takes some getting used to: you turn the easy, slick and consistently light steering through its 4.5 turns later than you might think when exiting junctions, to give the ample sides room to clear apexes. But the NBfL's flat sides mean that its mirrors are supremely effective at letting its driver judge clipping points and gaps. Get into a groove and there's real pleasure to be had from driving the NBfL smoothly and placing it accurately – even more so because the power delivery is so smooth. The brake pedal could use a little more feel for our taste, though.

The NBfL won't be cheap in full-scale production, but neither are its competitors: other hybrid double-deck buses cost £300,000, and when you consider the 12 to 15-year lifespan in London, the NBfL doesn't seem like such bad value.

The bus at speed and nicely ironing out the bumps. All windows have bonded glazing for greater structural rigidity. At this time the price being quoted for the bus was £330,000, but this later increased by 7½%.

Some of Wrightbus's double-deckers use a Volvo platform, but the NBfL is all its own work. The basic load-bearing structure is a steel backbone, to which is applied the aluminium superstructure and body. As can clearly be seen in the picture above, the turbodiesel generator is slung off the back of the chassis on pontoon rails, making access easy. The rest of the hybrid power train is beneath the rear seats near the back axle. It's possible that the basic design could spawn single-decked variants or even an open-roofed double-decker, but it won't happen for a while.

The NBfL may lack the outright visual charm of the original Routemaster, but we're confident that our capital's first new bus for 50 years is as postcard-friendly as it's possible to get. More significantly, though, the NBfL is a triumph of product design in an otherwise utterly unengaging and unromantic market.

Travelling on one may not quite revive the joy of holidays by charabanc but, then, nostalgia's not what it used to be, and the NBfL is a darned sight more pleasant to ride on and be around than any other modern bus we've encountered. What seals the NBfL's five-star rating is that it's as advanced under the body as it is interesting inside it. Clean, efficient and thought-provoking: it's public transport as it should be.

The easy access turbodiesel generator is mounted well to the rear of the back axle.

THE PROTOTYPES AT WORK

JOHN ALDRIDGE

The first bus stop in Graham Road, Hackney is just round the corner from busy Mare Street with its numerous shops. For any bus that has terminated in Hackney and laid-over in Clapton bus garage it is the first stop for picking up passengers. By 11am on 27th February 2012 the shelter at the stop begins to attract those who know that the first passenger service journey by the New Bus for London is scheduled to leave from it at midday. All the seats of the shelter are soon occupied, one end filled by two mothers with young children in pushchairs. Most other waiting passengers stand between it and the bus stop post. Many of them are older men and several seem to know each other – more so than you would expect at the average bus stop. As each bus on the 38, 242 and 277 pulls up, few people board but the crowd goes on growing. Some of those waiting are plainly puzzled by the two mothers who totally ignore all the buses. It transpires that they are local, just heard about the new bus, and thought they'd like a ride.

LT2 slowly leaves Clapton garage with plenty of staff observing the event at midday on 27th February 2012. At Leon Daniels's initiative, the bus carries white on black destination blinds – marking the start of a fleetwide move back towards these and an end to the Dayglo ones.

Printed notice announcing the vacancies for conductors on route 38. The first line of the job description suggests that the conductor would not be confined to the platform for the whole of each journey, but this is largely what happened in practice except where a wheelchair user needed assistance. There was understandable concern initially that the new buses did not get the adverse publicity of someone being badly injured in a platform accident. On route 38 LTs, all the conductors were also drivers. Their work was equally spilt between driving and conducting.

New Bus for London - Conductor

In February 2012 Arriva London will commence operation of the "New Bus for London", the first bus designed specifically for London's roads in more than fifty years.

This bus will operate with a crew of two drivers, one to drive the bus and the other to act as Conductor. Services will initially run from around 6am until around 8pm with a crew and then until midnight on a driver only basis, seven days a week. The bus will operate from Clapton/Ash Grove garage on route 38 and will initially operate in addition to the scheduled service although it will integrate into the full service in the future.

The role of Conductor is open to existing bus drivers and these staff will form a dedicated rota to operate the new buses.

Conductors will be required to:
- provide a supervisory / advisory role in respect of passenger activity on the bus, especially activity in the vicinity of the rear platform
- assist passengers in boarding / alighting as requested, particularly disabled passengers, or those with restricted mobility
- signal to the driver when boarding / alighting is complete
- providing passenger assistance and route, travel, fare and tourist information when safe to do so
- assist driver with the conversion of vehicle to / from crewed mode
- compile defect, quality or incident reports as requested
- complete fare validation checks as requested
- ensure their own working area remains Health & Safety compliant as well as exercising a duty of care to themselves and those around them in accordance with current legislation

Staff on the dedicated rota will work as both driver and as conductor interchangeably.

The successful applicants will be required to demonstrate strong customer service, communication and interpersonal skills and must be well presented at all times. Ideally, the candidates will have a good knowledge of London, both travel information and tourist information.

Staff who have been selected to work on the Olympic contracts will be excluded from this opportunity. Any staff who will transfer to other London Bus Operators under TUPE are also excluded.

Application Process
If you would like to be part of the NBfL team at Clapton/Ash Grove garage then submit an application on a staff memo to your Operating Manager by Saturday 10th March 2012. You will be required to undergo an assessment and interview process and your performance in your current role will form part of that assessment.

Arriva is committed to diversity. If you're good, you're welcome.

VACANCY

As noon approaches a bright red incident response van of London Buses draws up beyond the bus stop, as does a police car. A policeman appears and gently warns those standing on the kerb edge or in the road of the potential dangers and then leaves. They remain. Then a young woman in a high-viz jacket appears and shouts at them all to get back, but also leaves. Next, the driver of the van appears and tells those waiting that the bus has left the garage and is just out of sight round the corner. As LT2 hoves into sight he leaves. All three doors of the bus open and the crowd surges forward. Nobody could claim to be the first passenger! Unusually too there is not a great rush upstairs to gain the front seats, but a surprising number of people head to the rearward facing seats downstairs – usually the last seats to be occupied on a busy bus. There are many more of these seats than on other double-deckers and the enthusiasts and experts in the know are keen to see how the open rear platform and rear staircase work in practice – not that this is in any sense a normal journey. The ladies with children made a beeline for the wheelchair space behind the front stairs. Not everybody at the stop was able to get on and one keen and fit young man sprinted off ahead, and was able to board a couple of stops later. There is an absolute jumble of people downstairs, standing in every available space, and boarding was inhibited by several tv cameramen with their tripods and soundmen with microphones.

LT2 at the first bus stop of its first journey in service. People began to arrive about an hour beforehand and by the time the bus arrived the number of people hoping to board it exceeded its capacity.

Progress was slow, with long spells at stops while those trying to leave pick their way through the crowd. Other buses, including ordinary 38s, pass us. There is concern among the officials that while – as planned – the rear door remains open a warning buzzer sounds continually – which wasn't intended. There is a long stop at Islington station while the driver – an Arriva driving instructor – shuts down and then reboots the bus, with not much success. The software problem remains and it transpires the bus was only delivered to London the previous morning. Many passengers wrongly think the delay is caused by those wretched cameramen doing their interviews. One of them attempts to interview a child in one of the pushchairs. It promptly bursts into tears.

As the journey proceeds some impatient passengers leave, making way for others anxious to sample this bus. The ventilation system does not seem to be working properly and the upstairs windows have misted up. But people like the comfortable seats and the attractive interior. On battery drive the bus is impressively silent, but at the rear you can certainly hear the four-cylinder Cummins diesel engine, particularly when it first kicks in, with – like other hybrids – a rather agricultural noise.

As the bus approached many of the stops the rapid response van could be seen also. It was making spoiling moves to prevent a protest bus getting too close. A long Routemaster had been hired by the Transport Salaried Staffs Association, which was using it complete with large banners on the sides to protest about the new bus. Someone with a blond wig trying hard to look like Boris Johnson used a megaphone to shout the union's views.

The bus entered service only a couple of months before the mayoral election for which the Transport Salaried Staff Association's preferred candidate was Ken Livingstone, who had said that if elected he would scrap the project. It seemed extremely strange for a trade union to be opposing a project which would increase the number of staff employed. Here, a London Buses' Incident Reponse van tries to keep some distance between LT2 and the RML hired by the TSSA.

En route a surprisingly large number of pedestrians spotted the bus and quickly took pictures of it on their mobile phones. The bus was a good 30 minutes late by the time it reached Victoria bus station, where a huge crowd awaited. They occupied not only the adjacent bus stands but a fair part of the roadway too. And there were no bus station personnel telling them off. Patiently, after unloading, the bus drove round to the offside of Vauxhall Bridge Road, where it joined other buses laying over. It received some electronic or mechanical attention from another red van, and was initially joined by that Routemaster again as pseudo Boris m   'e another diatribe.

The Borismaster reappeared just before 3pm to return to Hackney, again fully loaded and again sometimes preceded and sometimes followed by the Routemaster with some more haranguing. This run was rather quicker, despite considerable traffic problems, and one further out-and-back run was completed later. Its first run had featured on lunch-time tv and radio, with inevitable descriptions of it as the new Routemaster. But no other bus ever, on its first day in trial service, can have had such a public start. It certainly contrasts with the first day of RM1 in service back in 1956. There had been newspaper stories about its debut, but public or even enthusiast interest was small and low key.

LT2 in Bloomsbury on its first journey in service. It was photographed and turned heads all along its route.

A large crowd greeted LT2 when it arrived at Victoria. In this view the bus is being driven for layover in Vauxhall Bridge Road.

Leaflets distributed by left-wing protesters, some of whom wore face masks, claimed that each bus cost £1.4m and that each passenger seated on board could instead have been bought a new BMW 3 series car. Similar claims that £11.4m had been spent on eight buses were made by opponents in news broadcasts. The protesters stand in front of LT2 while it is on layover in Vauxhall Bridge Road.

71

Passenger levels had become more normal for the second day's work for LT2. However, it usually ran only two or three of the five scheduled Monday to Friday round trips. Driver training and attention or checking by Wrightbus took up the rest of the days. The bus was driven by a driving instructor for the first few days, and then the standard procedure was for two drivers, one driving the other on the back platform alternately. They – and the LTs – were based at Arriva London's Ash Grove garage and provided a supplementary service that on paper was known as 38X and ran from Victoria to Hackney Central, just round the corner from Clapton garage, which was used for layovers. The normal 38 continued unchanged from Victoria to Clapton Pond, with about half the buses running only as far as Hackney Central and was worked from Clapton garage. For February and March LT2 was the solitary performer, LT1 having gone back to Wright's for modifications. It finally reappeared in London on 2nd April, and on Good Friday a few days later both buses were at work. But then gear-selection problems dogged LT1. When that was sorted it began what became quite a feature of life for some of the prototypes – visits to special events. LT1's began with the UK Coach Rally in Peterborough and the London Bus Museum's Spring Gathering at Wisley. Early June saw it in Wiltshire for the one day a year operation at the normally closed village of Imber.

Below A dusty LT1 at the military village of Imber on Salisbury Plain in June 2012 as part of a special bus running event.

Opposite upper LT1 at Guildhall in July 2012 for the Cart Marking Ceremony held each year by the Worshipful Company of Carmen.

Opposite lower LT3 on show at EuroBus Expo at the NEC Birmingham in November 2012.

In contrast to criticism in the press and on television, most ordinary passengers liked the bus, the comfort of its seats and interior décor. Its greatly improved suspension was noted by some. On the pavements and roads its reception was remarkable with residents as well as tourists keen to photograph it. One middle-aged, middle-class woman with a loud voice boarded one with her female companion, explaining that the bus was going the wrong way for their intended journey but she thought they ought to have a ride on it. The buses proved attractive to advertisers with all eight carrying adverts for West End shows such as *The Phantom of the Opera* and *The Lion King*: toy maker Corgi even produced versions of its 1:76 scale models carrying these different adverts.

Early January 2013 saw the buses begin to be used on Monday to Friday evenings in one-person form. Visits to various events continued, including LT7 at the Goodwood Festival of Speed and its inclusion in the BBCtv programme *Top Gear*, a 10-minute feature including a test drive through some narrow country lanes by the programme's James May. It was not until June that operations of the six remaining prototypes were incorporated into the regular schedules, and permanently operated in one-person form. This was for just six buses, because by this time LT1 and LT2 had begun a joint world tour, beginning with LT1 in New York and Boston, more of which later, and LT2 in Europe. Then in August LT3 went off to Hong Kong, leaving just five of the prototypes in London. This was further reduced to four in October when LT8 was returned to Wrightbus in Ballymena for trial modifications.

LT2 at Islington Green with conductor on board. It carried the special advert until July, when with the completion of delivery of all eight buses, the LTs received commercial advertising for West End shows. The advert reappeared on occasions when an LT was an exhibit at an event.

April 2012 had marked a turning point in securing the future of the class with the re-election of Boris Johnson as mayor of London for a second term. Official schedules for LT operation on the 38 had been available on the internet since before the start but at times were more a statement of hope. Next to arrive was LT6, which appeared in April, followed by LT4 in May. Originally the plans were for six operational prototypes, later changed to total eight. LT3 and LT5 were the last to be delivered in July, whereas LT7 had arrived in June, closely followed by LT8. A five-bus schedule had been introduced in June, at a time when there were only four LTs in the fleet! The schedule was for five buses on Mondays to Saturdays and four on Sundays. A seven-bus schedule was introduced from early August (7-5-3) and some days in October actually saw seven buses running. The reserved registrations for LTs 4-8 were not taken up, these buses receiving LT12DHT to LT12HHT.

From its earliest days the whole project attracted considerable media interest – and criticism. The most minor problems, such as the prototype running out of fuel on the M1 on a journey to the Millbrook test track, were adversely commented upon in a way experienced by no other bus type. The Green Party criticised the expense in a pseudo-calculation which assumed that London otherwise would not have needed to buy any new buses. Newspapers and tv news had plenty to say when a hot spell in summer 2012 saw high temperatures inside the buses: LT6 was returned to Ballymena for a month for tests and modifications.

This dusk view of LT1 at Victoria shows well the contrast in interior lighting between it and other London bus types. At Ash Grove, the buses soon developed a reputation for being less reliable than the Volvos. However, it has to be borne in mind that the new bus design, with its mix of tried and tested features and technical advances, was taken from concept to completion in a relatively short space of time. The number one priority was to have some running in service before the 2012 election.

Opposite The Goodwood Festival of Speed event in 2013 provided an opportunity to inspect the engine compartment of LT7. The 4.5 litre Cummins ISBe turbocharged engine drives a generator providing electricity to the Siemens permanent magnet motor which drives the rear axle. The generator and motor are upgradable to keep pace with future advances in technology. The bus is also equipped with a 75kWh lithium-ion battery pack which sits under the rear floor ahead of the nearside rear wheel. This battery pack uses braking energy and stores it to help the NBfL pull away from rest without using the engine/generator.

Left Beneath the higher stairs at the offside rear is the engine's radiator, equipped with four fans. The fuel tank is mounted towards the front of the bus, below the forward staircase. The fuel filler cap is behind a flap incorporated in a black panel that merges with the bus's glazing.

Below The LTs on route 38, which had been running as extras since introduction, were integrated into the main schedule on 15th June 2013. One week later, they were converted to full one-person operation and the drivers that had been acting as conductors for part of their duty returned to full time driving.

A BUS WITH POTENTIAL

KEITH McGILLIVRAY

As a Transport Planner, I believe as much should be done as possible to promote public transport, particularly in urban areas. With that in mind, it is worth recognising that the high profile arrival of the Borismaster has captured the attention of the general public in a manner that few other bus projects have. The design appeals to me, and after I first photographed the life-size mock up in the London Transport Museum in Covent Garden, I began to wonder how the style might look in other familiar liveries. Some readers might be familiar with a feature that appeared as an April Fool's item in *Buses* magazine in April 2013. The message behind the light-hearted story on that occasion was that outside London there might well be other applications for the vehicle and design. Further developing that idea, the computer-generated images included in this chapter show how the concept might look if applied to the city tours market or how it might look if applied to vehicle formats which are found in other bus markets throughout the world. When the bus was designed it was envisaged that it might be produced in different lengths and even open top versions and single deckers have not been ruled out. The trips overseas by LTs may perhaps generate some interest among bus operators in the countries being visited.

The Hong Kong bus market has been dominated by British designed vehicles for many years, with current designs from both Alexander Dennis and Wrightbus featuring strongly in recent deliveries. Examples of Wright's Gemini bodywork already feature in various fleets in Hong Kong suggesting some potential for the Borismaster concept to be applied there. This image shows one of the many attractive liveries that such vehicles might carry.

Several American and Canadian cities operate high capacity double-deck buses, and while there are examples of Alexander Dennis and Metsec vehicles, there are few, if any, Wrightbus examples. A version of this image initially featured in *Buses* magazine several months before Prince Harry and David Cameron accompanied LT1 on its visit to New York as part of the 'Innovation is Great' trade mission. This image, updated to include a version of the trade mission branding, shows how a range of safety features synonymous with North America might be incorporated into the Borismaster design.

Sightseeing tours represent significant business in cities worldwide, once operated by second-hand or cascaded service buses with open top roof conversions. Emerging accessibility, and more recently, air quality regulations have prompted operators to buy purpose-built vehicles and, in cities like London, a desire to maximise capacity has led to the appearance of tri-axle open toppers. This image shows how the staircase design feature might be incorporated to create an open topper, in this case in Big Bus Tours livery.

Australia, New Zealand and Singapore have shown increased interest in adopting higher-capacity double-deck vehicles, with Alexander Dennis developing a version of the Enviro500 for those markets. BusNSW, the bus and coach association for New South Wales, already operates a number of Custom-bodied tri-axle double deckers with twin forward steering axles. This image presented the opportunity to show how a Borismaster might look if operated by an independent, perhaps to a specification suitable for moving school children. Newlands of Wellington is understood to be one such operator with an interest in double-decker buses.

Perhaps the most well-known double-deck urban bus operation outside the UK is in Berlin, where more than 415 Neoman A39 Lion's City vehicles are in use. Like London, Berlin has tried to identify ways to overcome its own capacity problems and these buses can each accommodate 129 passengers. They are deployed on high capacity routes in Berlin, including the popular tourist route 100. Unlike modern day UK buses, Berlin's double-deckers are built to a low-height specification of 4.06m. This image shows how a low-height Borismaster might look if prepared for the BVG company in Berlin. BVG announced in 2013 that a grey skirt would no longer feature in its livery as a cost saving measure.

Bus routes which serve major airports are often operated by higher specification vehicles, helping to create a favourable first or last impression of a city. One means by which RATP might seek to provide a higher profile service to and from Paris Charles de Gaulle airport would be to replace articulated buses on the RoissyBus service with double-deckers. This image shows how a left-hand drive Borismaster might appear in such a guise – unlike the Berlin example, the bus is shown as full-height. While open rear platform operation may not be practical for an airport service, such a feature may otherwise be welcomed in Paris, reintroducing a concept that featured on more traditional buses there.

One motivation for the Borismaster project was to rid London's streets of articulated Mercedes Citaros which had been judged in some quarters to present problems with fares evasion and cyclist safety. A reluctance to fully embrace articulated buses leaves the UK as a relative outlier in the context of European bus operations, where there are differing attitudes to public transport provision and revenue protection. This has led some cities, in response to demands for increased capacity, to develop bi-articulated buses. This image, based on a Hess SwissTrolley 3, shows how a single deck, articulated Borismaster might look. It is portayed here in RATP livery, as though in use in Paris.

81

THE GREAT GLOBAL BUS TOUR

JAMES WHITING

In May 2013, LT1 arrived in the United States on the first leg of a year-long trade, tourism and goodwill tour that was scheduled to take in four continents and 16 countries including North and South America, India, Russia and South Korea. At a grand launch of the tour in New York, Prince Harry and PM David Cameron arrived on the bus after a tour in it of the city and stepped off to waiting crowds in Manhattan. 'What do you think of our bus?' asked Mr Cameron when greeting the head of Milk Studios, where he was one of those speaking about the importance of the USA and the UK working together to promote trade in the face of increasing competition from Asia. 'I love the bus,' came the reply, 'I like the wraparound at the back.' It was typical of the warm reception the bus was given in North America. Later in the month the bus took part in Internet Week New York (20-27 May) and the upper deck was fitted out for PowerPoint presentations.

Below Prince Harry and Prime Minister David Cameron leave the bus in Manhattan to take part in an event at New York's Milk Studios.

Opposite LT1 stands out from the crowd in downtown New York.

Below and opposite Two views of the bus at Times Square and one showing it parked in front of the United Nations building.

The bus then travelled to Boston, where it arrived on 29 May 'with full fanfare' according to a local report. Here it was scheduled to stop at every UK brand outlet in upmarket Newbury Street to celebrate all things British – and so it did, except one. Burberry's at one end of the street had to be skipped because First Lady Michelle Obama was campaigning next door for a Senate candidate – though surely she would have liked to see it! Those representing Britain in Boston included Conservative MP Nick De Bois and the British Consul General in Boston, Susie Kitchens. Support for the city following its terrorist bombings earlier in the year came by the bus visiting the site of the bombing. Following this second successful visit to a North American city, LT1 set of for Cartagena, Colombia – an up and coming tourist destination on the western coast of South America.

In Boston, the bus travels down Newbury Street, home of high quality shops including a number of British ones.

LT1's driver in New York and Boston was George Denning, in a uniform that probably did a good job of looking to the locals like a genuine London bus driver's outfit. With him here are MP Nick De Bois and Consul General Susie Kitchens.

LT1 crosses Charles River by traversing Harvard Bridge with a party of sightseers.

RIGHT BUS FOR LONDON?

GAVIN BOOTH

Transport for London is in a strong position to dictate what kind of buses run on its massive network. Although it owns only a very small proportion of the 7,500 buses providing its comprehensive service pattern, it does dictate basic specifications for those buses, including that double-deckers should have a centre exit door. London orders account for a significant proportion of new full-size bus deliveries and manufacturers have become well used to designing or adapting models with more than half an eye to orders from the contractors providing London services, and bodybuilders have become used to meeting TfL's exacting specifications. All of which has led observers around the country to pose the question: do we really need the New Bus for London or would off-the-peg buses do the job equally well?

Setting aside the controversial withdrawal of the Mercedes-Benz Citaro artics, there is no evidence to suggest that off-the-peg buses have been a disaster. Indeed, given that operating buses in central London can be particularly taxing, the fact that 97.6 per cent of the schedule was operated in 2012/13 and that excess wait time on high-frequency services was just one minute, then some might wonder, on the 'if it ain't broke' principle, why TfL did not stay with a successful formula.

London had led the move towards low-floor buses in the mid-1990s, and powered ahead to achieve an all-accessible fleet by 2005. It had started with small batches of low-floor single-deckers, bodied by Wrightbus in Ballymena, then a relatively minor player in the UK bus-building scene. When low-floor double-deckers came on line, London operators invested heavily in these and a London specification emerged, built by a range of bodybuilders on a number of different chassis types. Although these were Londonised buses, they were usually not too different from deliveries to operators in the rest of the country.

The main chassis suppliers were, initially DAF and Dennis, soon to be joined by Volvo and later by Scania, typically with bodywork by Alexander, East Lancs, Plaxton, Scania or Wrightbus. Subsequent ownership changes brought Alexander, Dennis and Plaxton together as Alexander Dennis, East Lancs into the Optare fold, and DAF's buses now carry the VDL name.

Although they are externally identical to double-deckers supplied to operators around the UK, the London deliveries incorporate features rarely seen elsewhere, like a separate exit door, and as a consequence of this a relatively low number of lower deck seats. Where a 10.4m-long Volvo B9TL/Wright Gemini in Go-Ahead's London fleet has seats for just 62 passengers, a single-door example in the same group's Brighton & Hove company has 71 seats with 28 rather than just 21 on the lower deck, giving more provision for less able passengers.

The specification of London's off-the-peg double-deckers has evolved and while passengers from other parts of the UK may find the interior layout unfamiliar to them, it is clearly what TfL deems necessary for London's apparently unique operating conditions. A separate exit door makes a great deal of sense in speeding up passenger flow, yet outside London even the once most fervent advocates of two-door buses have moved to a single-door layout, usually citing the increase in the number of exit door accidents and insurance claims; a proportion of these were spurious, but the cost of dealing with them drove other urban operators back to single doors, very quickly in the case of Manchester and Birmingham, where the local authority fleets had pioneered the use of dual doors to help speed driver-only operation only to find problems with passengers getting caught in doors, delays as drivers checked the centre doors, and passengers using these doors to avoid paying a fare. Even Lothian Buses, which specified dual-door buses until 2001, decided that the cost of insurance claims outweighed any time advantage at busy Edinburgh stops.

The low seating capacity in the lower deck of London buses has been a bone of contention with passengers, particularly those who are looking for a seat on the low-floor section rather than climbing up on to a pedestal-mounted seat. The New Bus has the same number of seats, ten, in the low-floor area of the lower deck as the Volvo/Wright Gemini buses that operate in London. The number of forward-facing seats, generally preferred by passengers, is lower though – 14 on the LT while the latest Gemini has 21.

The most familiar off-the-peg buses on London's streets today, the ADL Enviro400 and the Wright Gemini, are attractive and distinctive products, but represent evolution rather than the revolution that is the NBfL Alexander Dennis and Volvo have been the main suppliers of London's growing fleet of diesel-electric hybrid double-deckers and have the most to lose as TfL receives its ongoing deliveries of LTs.

The sight of several 24s in Trafalgar Square was confirmation that the New Bus had arrived and they really stood out from the herd. On my visit, it was the hottest day of the year and a few days previously the buses had been dubbed 'cauldrons on wheels' as the upper-deck temperature hit over 30°C, criticising the air chill installation and lack of opening windows. These, said TfL, were 'teething problems'. NBfL designer Thomas Heatherwick has said that he wanted opening windows but was overruled.

The air-chilling was working hard on the 24s I sampled, and seemed to be doing the job, if a touch noisily. What did impress, though, was the comfort of the ride, which was at least as good as the best off-the-peg buses, helped perhaps by the long wheelbase, low build and the engine position under the rear staircase. The retro look of the interior is attractive and welcoming, but on closer examination you realise just how much thought has gone into the layout, fittings and furnishings. The 'old-style' bus seats look very different to the modular seats fitted to most buses these days, yet when you use them you quickly appreciate the shaped seat back that helps to define 'your' half of the seat. And the deep cushions are an antidote to moves by some operators to cut back on seat cushioning, while the moquette has a traditional look without being in any way old-fashioned or a pastiche of earlier designs. Heatherwick has provided lighting that is subtle and effective, providing a balanced and more restful level of illumination at night.

LT20 looks very much at home as it negotiates the Sunday afternoon Camden Market crowds.

There have been criticisms that the upper deck feels claustrophobic and it can seem this way, particularly to passengers used to the deep windows and arched roof of Gemini bodies. The upper deck windows on the LT are certainly shallower (at 24ins) than on the Gemini (35½ins) but they do afford an excellent view for seated passengers. The upper deck headroom is also less than on most other buses, though the Geminis fitted with air cooling equipment and ducts have a similar headroom below these as the LT. It is in the rear section of the lower deck that headroom is a bit of a problem, being between two and three inches less than in the Gemini. Taller people need to take care when leaving the seats in this area.

At the Ballymena launch, Thomas Heatherwick had explained to me that his company had to learn about buses very quickly and he was able to question many of the long-accepted shibboleths of bus design. 'The bus had to look and feel good, but it also had to be comfortable', he said. 'The materials we used were led by the push to minimise energy use and keep weight down. Everything was designed from scratch – we didn't just take material from the parts bin and make it fit.

'From the outside, people will be able to see people moving around in the bus, as the glazing follows the passenger flow. We went for shallower windows upstairs to avoid problems of overheating in the summer, and nobody should need deep windows as they won't be standing. Travelling upstairs in a bus is a great experience, the cheapest high-quality view on the world.

Comparing the upper deck interior of a Gemini body (left) with the NBfL shows that while the Gemini boasts deeper windows and more conventional lighting, the LT on the right is different but effective.

'We wanted the lighting to be warm, and not the unflattering and uncalming fluorescent tubes that would be more at home in a piggery, so we are using low-energy LED lights. We are trying to reintroduce the "specialness" of travelling by bus, taking into account all the rules, regulations and directives that have been introduce in the half-century since London last commissioned a bus for its streets.'

The raised seats at the rear of the lower deck offer a good view forward – or backward, if, as I did, you want to watch how passengers interact with the conductor on the rear platform.

But the long wheelbase and the overall length of 11.3m could cause problems; two very sharp corners at the Pimlico end of the 24 route require careful negotiation, and nobody would pretend that the NBfL could ever be as nippy as its distinguished Routemaster predecessor, although its speed between stops on straight roads is impressive where traffic allows.

There has been much mumbling about the cost of the New Bus, but at £354,000 each for a bus bristling with new features is not a great deal more than an off-the-peg hybrid. The development costs of around £11million were used mischievously by some to suggest that the eight prototypes were costing £1.375million each, and if the bus had been stillborn at this stage there might have been some justification, but every manufacturer incurs development costs for each new model and these are recouped from subsequent sales. When you consider the long gestation period of the Routemaster, TfL, the designers and Wrightbus have done remarkably well to take the NBfL from an idea to full production in just three years.

The driver of LT23 negotiates the left turn at St George's Square, Pimlico where the traffic island was moved one metre off centre to allow the new buses to make this manoeuvre. The next longest double-deckers in TfL service are the Scania OmniCitys which are 10.8 metres. Most Gemini 2s are 10.4 metres long and the Enviro400s 10.1 metres.

The theory of three doors speeding up the service has not always proved to be realised in practice. Confusion about which door to use has slowed the bus at bus stops – partly caused by the fact that in central London the buses often have to pull up with the front entrance by the bus stop; the other entrances are frequently ignored. The tendency for tourists to ask the driver questions also hold things up. In the case illustrated here, the driver – with commendable politeness – spent three minutes answering the group's questions.

Diversions are common in central London and causes including road works, demonstrations and state visits. Here LT18 has been diverted away from the eastern end of Victoria Street to run via Horseferry Road. Account needs to be taken of the extra length of the buses on such occasions. In the reverse direction for this diversion, 24s ran the full length of Horseferry Road to run via Millbank to reach Parliament Square. Other services reached Victoria Street by turning left into Marsham Street.

There are still big questions to consider – does it work, what does it cost to run, is it more costly to run than an off-the-peg bus? The cost of providing a conductor is one that conventional London buses avoid, but from observation the conductors perform a useful role, helping passengers, especially less able ones, looking after their safety around the rear platform and encouraging passengers to use all three doors for boarding and alighting.

TfL has been guarded about the fuel consumption of NBfL, saying it expected to release details 'when a statistically robust sample of production vehicles have been in service for at least six months'. Responding to a Freedom of Information request, TfL said that fuel consumption achieved during the TfL simulated route test cycle at the Millbrook facility was 11.7mpg which, it said, 'provides a like-for-like comparison with similar double-deck vehicles under identical conditions, carried out by an independent evaluation facility'. Further FoI enquiries revealed that the eight prototypes had achieved a fleet average of 6.74mpg, which TfL said was significantly better than the standard diesel buses operating on route 38, and expected the production buses to deliver approximately 1mpg improvement on the prototypes.

TfL figures from a study of its existing hybrids show that both ADL and Volvo hybrids achieve very similar average mpg of 7.2mpg, with the hybrids previously used on the 24 route averaging 6.6mpg. If the LT can achieve the 7.74mpg it suggests, then this would go some way to justifying the initial costs of the bus. Compare this with the 6.1mpg TfL quotes for hybrid double-deckers on the 73 route, and the 5.3mpg for diesel buses on the same route, then the LT will provide significant fuel savings and contribute greatly to a cleaner London over their estimated 14-year life. The unladen weight of the LT was another concern, but the designers have ensured that the greater length LTs weigh much the same as some contemporary Volvo/Geminis. The LTs introduced on the 11 were the first to match the heaviest of the Geminis, at 12320kg, and the lower passenger capacity of the LTs is explained by an increase in the passenger notional weight since the Geminis were licensed. Newly delivered buses of 12320kg can legally carry a maximum of 82 passengers (the conductor is not included in the calculation). Both types are 5–6 per cent heavier than the ADL Enviro400s.

Of course an advanced bus like this brings new challenges for engineers, who have to deal with sophisticated electronics and adapt their maintenance regimes to deal with this very different animal, but as it is rolled out in squadron service this will surely become easier to handle.

For passengers, most importantly, it seems to be a success. Passengers I spoke to on the 24 liked the look and feel of the LTs and visitors and locals alike enjoyed the chance to use the open rear platform at stops and when the bus was caught in traffic. I am happy to admit that I am a convert to the New Bus for London. From initial scepticism – why do they need this when ADL and Volvo can supply perfectly good hybrids? – I was won over by the way the bus looks, the ride, the interior décor, and feel that TfL, Heatherwick Studios and Wrightbus have combined to produce an important new type for London – maybe just for London so far as the UK is concerned, though I would guess some of its design features might appear on other buses. By the middle of the century London's then mayor will probably be under pressure to develop an equally iconic successor.

Opposite Buses trapped in traffic and passengers trapped on buses – but not with the conductor-operated New Bus for London, where passengers can check and freely hop off where necessary.

THE BUS IN PRODUCTION

JAMES WHITING

Following the completion of delivery, in July 2012, of the eight prototypes and re-election of Boris Johnson, an order was placed with Wrightbus in September 2012 for 600 further LTs. Approval for this was given by the TfL board on the 20th. It was anticipated that the first batch of 30 buses would enter service by the end of the following April, though at the time the first route to have the production vehicles had not been finalised. As part of the contract between Wrights and TfL, which envisaged 127 LTs being delivered in 2013, 270 in 2014, 184 in 2015 and 19 in 2016, another 400 need to be ordered before another manufacturer can be invited to tender. If the bus has a manufacturing life beyond 2016 dual sourcing would become possible.

The nice touch, at Hendy's initiative, of Northern Ireland registration numbers to accord with the fleet numbers of the buses gives a clue to the size of the fleet he would like to see, for he requested the reservation of 3,000 marks for 3,000 LTs. This was refused by the DVLA in Belfast but it did allocate matching numbers to cover the 600 on order. Whether more than 600 are ever built is largely dependent on the attitude of a new mayor in 2016 to a bus that is indelibly associated with Boris Johnson.

In a break from the system that had been in place since route tendering began, the buses would be owned by Transport for London and supplied to the operating companies on a notional lease. It was almost inevitable that this would be the case for a number of reasons. Commercial leasing companies had come off badly from the early withdrawal of the bendy buses and the difficulty in finding new customers for them (some ended up in Malta, where engine fires were again to be a problem). Undoubtedly then, their leasing charges for a bus that no-one else in the UK was likely to want would have been high. The bus operators would be unwilling to be responsible for a new bus that their engineers had not specified nor for the financial penalties that would apply for buses being out of service for mechanical reasons. TfL owning the buses was realistically the only option.

It was an arrangement which, though initially a large financial burden on TfL of over £200m, was expected to save money in the long term. It would also enable the buses to be easily moved between operators as route contracts changed. Indeed such a move would be unnoticed by most passengers, as the conductors would move also. The leases contain clauses to ensure that the LTs are maintained to a standard that would not place obstacles to this. Maintenance of the buses is the responsibility of the operating companies, which are however able to subcontract the work to Wrightbus at a TfL-negotiated price as is provided for in TfL's contract with that company. The contract specifies that spare parts for the buses will be available for 29 years (ie until 2045 in respect of the order for 600), made up of 14 years of anticipated service in London and 15 years thereafter. Annual mileage for each bus is assumed to be 56,000.

Opposite LT17 has been brought from Ballymena to pose for the official opening on 10th May 2013 of Wright's new chassis plant in Antrim, which began producing chassis for the new bus in April 2013, that for LT32 being the first. LT17 carries the registration intended for LT1 for the occasion. Outside, further completed buses are lined up for the photographers present. The matching registration numbers on the production LTs certainly make identification of the buses easier for staff. Whilst associating 1 to 8 with the first to eighth letters of the alphabet may have made LTs 1-8 (L61AHT to L12HHT) identifiable from a distance, anything beyond eight (with a jump to JHT) would not have been very helpful.

Production of the 600 LTs began at Ballymena around the time the contract was placed and in April 2013, when the first buses left the factory, it was announced that route 24 would be the first to receive the buses, on which they would enter service on 22nd June. Twenty-seven buses would be allocated to Holloway garage plus five spares. The aim was to convert at least two and possibly three routes in 2013, ruling out a full conversion of the 38, the 73 or indeed any other routes needing more than 30-35 buses. A number of routes in this category were considered and surveyed, including the 9, 11, 19, 23, 24, 88, 94, 168, 189 and 390. Among the other factors governing the choice of the earliest services for the buses was the desire for them to be visible in many different parts of central London. In the event four routes were selected to receive LTs before the end of 2013, the 24, 11, 9 and 390 in that order.

The driver's cab area is in the foreground of this view of one of the chassis being worked on at the Wrightbus Antrim factory.

Below left Holes in the panelling of the production vehicles are among the measures introduced to save weight.

Below right LT13 at Metroline's Cricklewood garage during training of conductors for the 24. Training was split between classroom and on the road.

The selection and the training of staff to be conductors on the buses were the responsibility of the operator. The contracts were amended so that the total cost of training and employing the extra staff member was covered by TfL. Pay was £9.30 per hour basic, £9.80 for weekend work and £10 per hour for overtime. Training of conductors (or customer assistants) for the 24 was carried out by Metroline at Cricklewood garage and on the route over a three-week period ending on 21st June. The training included trips along the route in a bus with other conductors to learn about places of interest and gain some familiarity with the bus stops. It was also important to be fully familiar with those controls on the bus that the conductors would be responsible for, the types of question they might be asked and the handling of passengers in wheelchairs.

Successful applicants would be those with good customer service skills (exemplified by the volunteers at the previous year's Olympic Games), a good knowledge of Underground and bus routes and very good spoken and written English. The great majority of appointments for the 24 were full time, with four part-time staff. During the week before the route was converted to LTs, the buses destined for Holloway garage were assembled at Perivale ready to be driven to the garage on the evening of the 21st. The following day, after a gap of 7½ years, two-person operated buses would be running in normal service on a London route.

The drivers, each of whom was given 12 hours familiarisation on the new bus, have ultimate responsibility for the safety of passengers. The conductor's main job is to safeguard passengers boarding and alighting at the rear platform. The conductor signals to the driver that the rear platform is clear and the bus's handbrake is not released until this signal is given. As on conventional buses, the driver is responsible for checking the centre doors by means of ceiling mounted mirrors in the saloon and cctv in the cab. The public address is also in his charge.

CUSTOMER ASSISTANTS

Are you a unique performer? Do you have the ability to play to an audience? Do you really care about the customer experience? Do you want to be involved in a unique opportunity in Central London?

Metroline will be showcasing to the world when its route 24 becomes the first route in London to be converted to the New Bus for London.

We are looking for unique people that can become the life and soul of the route 24 as it travels through some of the most magnificent sites in London.

Full and part time vacancies available. In your written application, please tell us about your availability. Games maker qualities are essential!

Responsibilities will include:
- Providing general customer assistance with route, travel and tourist information.
- Providing assistance to wheelchair and buggy users
- Providing a visible presence in the vehicle to customers
- Ensuring customers board and alight the vehicle in safety.

Left Part of the advert for conductor jobs on route 24. With this conversion, the official terminology for the second crew member changed to 'customer assistant' to reflect the fact that they did not collect fares. This did not stop most people referring to them as conductors.

Overleaf On Thursday 20th June, the LTs for route 24 are lined up ready at Perivale and are having their exterior adverts fitted. The following night they will be driven to Holloway ready for service on the Saturday. LT15 was delivered carrying the registration number for LT22, which LT22 also carried. This was corrected before the buses entered service.

LTs on the 24 did not get off to a good start on 22nd June 2013. In the weeks preceding, a house to house delivery of eight-page fold out postcards was undertaken to sing the praises of the new bus. In theory there was much to be praised, but in practice the service provided in the first few days was a substantial drop in quality compared with the service the people along the route had been receiving with the buses previously used.

As the 24 route operates 24 hours a day the first LT journey from Hampstead Heath coincided with the transition from opo to crew operation and left on time at 6.56am, driven by Surface Transport Managing Director Leon Daniels, arriving at Pimlico about 25 minutes late and back at Hampstead Heath at the end of the first round trip almost an hour late. The main cause of delays seems to have been the unfamiliarity of passengers with the boarding and alighting arrangements at bus stops, but road works in Victoria Street also contributed. This late running was to continue all through the day with drivers recording serious delays, leading to curtailed journeys. It probably did not help that the Northern Line paralleling the 24 was closed for engineering works that weekend. A few of the buses had problems with the door alarm systems (as had been the case with the very first LT journey on route 38) and there were a number of other breakdowns. Extended intervals and bunching were therefore inevitable.

A number of VIPs were present for the first journey, the bus selected for this honour being LT32. Apart from Leon Daniels in the driving seat for the first trip, Metroline's CEO Jaspal Singh, its Chief Operating Officer Sean O'Shea and Holloway garage's chief engineer were joined by Mike Weston (Operations Director London Buses) at Holloway garage for the bus to make its way to the Hampstead Heath terminus for its first trip to Pimlico. Sir Peter Hendy (knighted in the New Year's honours 2013) joined the bus at the Pimlico end and the bus's designer Thomas Heatherwick joined at Hampstead after its return, travelling on it as far as Tottenham Court Road on the second journey to Pimlico, which had Sir Peter at the wheel; Leon then resumed driving for the return trip to Hampstead Heath and the end of the first half of the duty.

LT32 picks up passengers for the very first journey on Saturday morning, including one young boy who had reportedly been waiting for two hours so he could be first on the bus. Leon Daniels is driving. Despite being the day after the summer solstice and two days before midsummer, 22nd June was not a warm day so the cooling problems that were later to manifest did not become evident.

A factor with the LTs may be that the prototypes at Ash Grove were maintained by a member of Wright's staff who was in attendance four days a week, whereas at Holloway that garage's engineering staff took a greater role and the engineering specification was a big shift from what they had been used to with other buses at the garage. Daniels publicly praised the Metroline engineers for coping as they did. One that I spoke to said there were 'too many electrics on the bus'. Problems reported in the first few days included electrical malfunctions, engine or battery overheating and power steering failures. In some buses, ceiling panels were coming away in service.

A big effort was made by all concerned to sort out why so many buses were breaking down – at least six were noted on the first Monday of operation – problems with the sophisticated electrics and power steering failures being among the main issues. Then, later in the month when the temperatures in London rose, it became apparent that the air-cooling system was not working effectively. Press references to the buses being 'saunas' or 'cauldrons' prompted another urgent investigation into what was happening. On the 38, the LTs also led to complaints about the inadequacy of the ventilation but the buses had been extras to the normal schedule, so on very hot days they could return to the garage. It is surprising however that the air-cooling problems had to reach such a high public profile before they were properly addressed. BBC London news reported in mid-September that consideration was being given to adding opening windows in the lower deck on future deliveries of the bus.

On the first Monday of operation, in common with a number of other LTs, LT24 has broken down. According to the driver, the power steering has failed. The rescue truck has arrived in Charing Cross Road to take it back to Holloway garage but first the recovery mechanic takes a look underneath. For its tow, the bus will be lowered sufficiently to give adequate clearance at the back.

Assisting wheelchair passengers is an important part of the conductor's job. It is one that needs to be carried out sensitively as some of those in wheelchairs welcome the assistance while others insist on being independent. A shorter and two-door version of the bus, if retaining the rear door, would need to provide for wheelchairs to enter via the front entrance.

Holloway garage had an open day on Saturday 10th August and there was an opportunity to travel on an LT along the route taken by the buses to reach the 24 terminus at Hampstead Heath – via Tufnell Park, Kentish Town, Prince of Wales Road and then line of route to the terminus. Route number 639 was displayed in the windscreen and the bus used was LT24, which had taken part in the annual Imber event the previous Saturday. It still carried its special Imber route advertising, which it continued to do for some time after – much to the bemusement no doubt of any Londoners who noticed it.

Following an *Evening Standard* front page headline about the 'Sweltering Boris Buses' on Friday 5th July, a weekend of intensive attempts to solve the problem took place. The following Wednesday, the *Standard* reported that 'London's transport commissioner today vowed that problems with soaring temperatures on the new Boris bus had been solved'. It went on to report that 'Sir Peter Hendy and designer Thomas Heatherwick were spotted last night with thermometers testing the heat in an empty bus as it circled Kings Cross', the workplace and home of Heatherwick. Perhaps they were lucky with the bus they sampled, or perhaps an empty bus at night might not give a good impression of how it might be at midday with a good load of passengers. Either way, the problem had not been solved and the following week a company that had not previously been involved with the bus, Birmingham-based Grayson Thermal Systems, was appointed by Wrightbus to get things sorted. A programme was quickly drawn up, the work on each bus taking the best part of a week.

Wrightbus made progressive improvements in the weight of the LTs during the latter half 2013 so that they could move closer to the specified capacity of 87 passengers. The weight reductions were achieved by the measure illustrated on page 98 and by using lighter materials where possible. The LTs on route 24 (LTs 9-40) were 12460kg and could legally carry 80. Those delivered for the 11 (LTs 41-68) were labelled as 12320kg and had a legal limit of 82 passengers and those delivered for route 9 (LTs 69-94) were 12200kg and could carry 84 legally. LTs 95-117, for route 390, are slightly heavier at 12220kg but have the same legal load as LTs 69-94. In the calculation of the maximum load the conductor is not counted, so the capacity is the same whether or not there is one on board.

The heating and cooling system on the LTs was specified in the contract to keep the inside temperature between 15 and 21 degrees, but temperatures above 30 degrees were recorded. On one of the hot summer days of 2013 a Routemaster overtakes LT18 to give a comparison of rear ends and a good impression of the new bus's highly reflective tinted glass.

Ceiling panels coming loose, graffiti on seat handrails and broken light fittings were among the problems inside the production buses.

Below This dashboard-mounted unit on a Holloway LT is a braking monitor, which enables the driver to raise awareness of how professionally he or she is using the brakes. From two shades of green, through two shades of yellow to red, the aim is to keep the yellow and red lights unlit as much as possible. The results are recorded and can be viewed by the driver (and supervisor) back at the garage. If the braking falls below a set standard the driver has to have retraining. The monitoring was taken a step further with route 11's LTs, which were fitted with RIBAS instruments to check excessive Revving, Idling, Braking, Acceleration and Speed.

The buses were reported to be falling short in their fuel consumption and emissions figures, in some cases worryingly. At the start of each day the batteries are fully charged and, each time they fall to 40% charge, the engine is designed to start automatically and run until they are fully charged again. It is the engine stop-start technology of hybrids that reduces fuel requirements and in the case of the LTs they were designed to achieve a 40 per cent saving in fuel. In practice, though, at least some of the engines were running for a greater part, and sometimes a much greater part, of each trip than had been intended. The emissions were causing particular concern because of the bus's 'green' aspirations.

This staircase leads to an open platform

Watch out for moving traffic

Cyclists Stay back

The bus at its best. The neat bench seating and the stylish lighting set the LT apart.

Left Necessary notices in and around the bus. The number of stickers came in for criticism from some quarters but it is not much greater than on other modern buses.

Route 11 was selected as the second route to be fully converted to LT operation and was scheduled for phased conversion from Saturday 21st September. Conductors were trained, like those with Metroline, in four groups which each spent ten days on the road and five days in the classroom. Training began on 2nd September and the last new conductors completed their training on the Tuesday following the first buses starting on the 11, but by the time the first one entered service on the evening of Friday 20th September the target for completion of the changeover had slipped from Wednesday 25th to the middle of the following week; it subsequently slipped further. The first day the morning run-out on the 11 was 100% LTs was 15th October. The period of over three weeks taken for this conversion suggests the buses may have been undergoing engineering attention.

The conductors on the 11 were each equipped with iPads. With these, they can sign on to begin their duties at Fulham Broadway, the Victoria Coach Station eastbound or westbound stops or Liverpool Street (all 24 conductors sign on at the Hampstead Heath terminus, where there is a facility in the staff hut there). The iPads also contain details of their duty rota, travel enquiry information and a form for reporting any incidents. As with Metroline, applications from people with experience in customer service and retail work made up a good proportion of those who were successful. One of the conductors on the 11 was formerly an air steward.

On the first weekend of LTs on route 11, LT42 is followed by WVL130 in Whitehall. A phased changeover had been planned, but the timescale was greater than had been intended.

Not only are the customer assistants not able to take fares, they are trained not to get into arguments with anyone who refuses to touch in their Oyster card or show a pass. One passenger I saw doing just this got the response: 'If revenue gets on mate, it's your fine not mine'. In the first few days of the 11, revenue inspectors were more in evidence than they had been in the first few days of the 24, suggesting some degree of fare loss was being suffered on conversion to LT. The presence of a second member of staff does however make it more likely that someone will pay their fare than running a bus with three possible points of entry with driver only. The conductors are a very popular feature, dealing with a variety of situations in a friendly and efficient way. In the first three months of the 24 there had been no formal compensation claims involving conductors, though there had been a few cases of minor platform accidents. It was only a matter of time before a serious incident and on 4th October a woman fell off a 24 and sustained a head injury that was initially life threatening.

A few days before the 11 started, customer assistants at Holloway garage began to receive the first elements of their uniform. They were also given name badges in a modern incarnation of the 20th century PSV badges which showed the conductor's number. Then, route 11 conductors started to receive badges soon after they began work, these ones showing their names in all capital letters in contrast with those on Metroline.

The recruits for the 24 were told that 9,000 people had approached the company to apply for the job, including 800-900 from one advert in the Metro newspaper alone. The 11 attracted 2,500 enquiries before applications closed on 19th July. Of these, 250 were selected from their CVs, whittled down through a process of group interview and one to one interview to select the 57 conductors needed. Two of the best ambassadors for London buses are seen here. Route 11's conductors were trained to stand by the door, as seen in the second view, but by November they had moved to the conventional position as on other routes.

On its second day in service, at around 1pm on Sunday 22nd September, LT62 was involved in a serious accident while operating on route 11. As the bus approached the traffic lights at the junction of Lower Sloane Street and Pimlico Road, the driver is reported to have had a problem with the brakes. The bus continued 'at speed' past the red traffic lights and along Chelsea Bridge Road until colliding with a car and crashing into the back of a single-deck bus on route 360. The driver of the LT and the two occupants of the car were taken to hospital with serious injuries and it is very fortunate that no-one was killed. The conductor (who acted commendably and calmly to warn those on board to prepare for an impact) and 12 passengers suffered bruising but no major harm. An immediate investigation was set up and a team of engineers urgently sent to check out the other LTs at Stockwell garage. The conductor of the crashed bus, who had suffered a bruised back, was at work again on the Tuesday, accompanied by another fully trained customer assistant to enable her to rest as needed. As the new buses were falling behind in being available for service over half of the trained conductors had no work to do immediately but were of course paid.

The conversion following route 11, that of route 9, was carried out in one go on Saturday 26th October 2013. It was operated with conductors on Mondays to Fridays only. The same applied to the next route, the 390, in December, when route 24 changed from daily operation with conductors to Monday to Friday only. Then it became known that the first conversion of 2014, route 148, would be one-person operated at all times. Another development was a trial reinstatement of conductors on route 38 from 4th November. The trial, on Mondays to Fridays involved switching from two-person operation to opo, or vice versa, during the journey, the switchover point being Mildmay Park. Four Ash Grove drivers were persuaded to volunteer to be conductors on the basis that it was for four weeks only. The times of the duties, all of which started and finished at Mildmay Park, were: 1014-1205 and 1545-1939; 0836-1331 and 1724-1915; 0719-1120 and 1225-1642; 0705-1055 and 1205-1615, giving two morning peak hour journeys serving

central London with conductors and two evening peak hour trips. The operation of shutting and locking the rear doors can be done in less than a minute, as can the unlocking and opening in the reverse direction. The trial opened up the possibility of having conductors on parts of routes only, a sensible development that would make the best use of the second on-board staff member. The existence of the rear door also means that if a conductor is delayed getting to his or her bus, the bus can continue in service in opo mode.

At the start of this book on the New Bus for London it was recorded that there were many who doubted the wisdom of the whole project. Boris Johnson's dream had been to provide around 600 new hop on, hop off updates of the Routemaster. To TfL it was an opportunity for a new technically advanced bus with green credentials substantially surpassing other double-deckers running in London. Two years after the first prototype was launched, there were still those who questioned what the New Bus for London was for, but the bus remains a beautiful addition to the capital's streets.

By the time of route 9's conversion, the buses were running more reliably, with fewer breakdowns being noted. LT 84 is seen in Pall Mall. Route 9 being one of the two heritage routes, the hop on, hop off facility was provided by RMs seven days a week for most of its length.

On 11th November 2013, as part of Remembrance Day commemorations, RML903 ran on route 24 alongside the LTs. The Routemaster is seen with LT20 at Pimlico. RML903 was scheduled to meet Sir Peter Hendy's RM1005 (on route 211) in Whitehall at 11am.

PICTURE CREDITS

Alexander Dennis Ltd 25 top
Alexander Dennis Ltd and Capoco Design Ltd 24
Alexander Dennis Ltd and Foster + Partners 23
Chris Ashby 17 bottom
Aston Martin and Foster + Partners 11 (courtesy TfL), 12
David Bell 55 bottom
Terry Blackman 56, 57, 73 top
Gavin Booth 46, 47, 48, 49, 90
British Consulate General, Boston 86, 87
British Consulate General, New York 83, 84, 85
Capoco Design Ltd 9, 10
John Connell 29
Evening Standard 69
Richard Godfrey 74
Haymarket Media Group Ltd 37, 60, 61, 62, 63, 64, 65
Hilton Holloway 41, 43, 44
Hilton Holloway and Lineale Design 18
Ian Jordan 52, 77 bottom
Mark Kehoe 30/31, 32, 33, 34, 35 bottom, 76, 105
Mark Lyons 111
Jamie Martin Design 13 top
Keith McGillivray 36, 75, 78, 79, 80, 81
Alan Millar 50/51, 70, 72, 97, 98 top and bottom left
Raj Nahal 15 bottom
Press Association 82, 110, jacket
Jukka Rautiainen 17 top
Reiko Ito 16
Doug Rose This page
Jimmy Sheng 98 bottom right
Kevin Smith 66, 68, 102, 108
Colin Stannard Title page spread
TfL Press Office 27
Times Newspapers Ltd 100/101
Toby Tinsley 14
Pope Wainwright 15 top
Russell Young 53 bottom left

If not otherwise credited above, photographs in this book are copyright Capital Transport and drawings are by Ivan Frontani